Don Cupitt

The Religion of Being

SCM PRESS LTD

0 334 02731 4

First published 1998
by SCM Press Ltd
9–17 St Albans Place, London N1 0NX

Typeset at Regent Typesetting, London
and printed in Great Britain by
Biddles Ltd, Guildford and King's Lynn

For Susan

Contents

Introduction:
The story so far . . .

During the 1990s I have been trying to work out a new philosophy and a new account of the religious life. So far, perhaps the shortest and clearest statements have been those given in the three essays of 1994/5 – *After All*, *The Last Philosophy*, and *Solar Ethics*.[1] But often I find that my own ideas are to me just as objectionable and hard to understand as other people find them; and in any case philosophy is an elusive and perverse subject. Just when you think you have achieved an all-round clear view of a problem, a whole new angle that you hadn't thought of opens up. The present book has arisen, then, because I have found a big gap that needs to be filled. The argument has to be pushed on another stage, for I need to tackle the question of Being.

In some quarters the information that I have been working on a book about Being has been received with a certain amount of hilarity. 'That shouldn't take long, eh?' Comparisons have been made with a book by Tony Blair about socialism, or by Gordon Brown about humour. But here I shall neither name names, nor repeat all the jokes. Certainly not. *Everyone* agrees that there are true statements in the indicative mood, and therefore that there is something that such statements are about; so that the question of Being arises for people whose universe is as ultralight as Nagarjuna's, just as much as it does for people whose universe is as thick and densely-packed as Aristotle's. Aristotle was so grossly Western and materialistic that he did not believe there could be such a thing as a vacuum in Nature, and Nagarjuna was so ultralight an Eastern Buddhist philosopher that his world is utterly Empty, with no solid stuff in it at all. Nevertheless, widely though they differ, they do each have a world; and so do we. The question of Being always arises. Indeed, the question: 'What is Being, in us, and for us? What is real; what is it *to be*?' presses upon all of us particularly acutely today. By engaging with it, I may be able to get clearer about what I have been doing in the past decade or so, and what new kind of religious life I have been trying to commend.

The new point of view has been described since *Creation out of Nothing* (1990) as 'expressionist'. This means that I see the exemplary human being as an artist. We are bundles of often-discordant forces, all of them struggling for expression. Indeed, our whole life is a struggle for expression, through which we are trying to become ourselves by unifying ourselves. For this we need unifying symbols, channels of expression that can carry different forces and different messages simultaneously; and such channels are indeed supplied by our various socially-evolved symbol-systems. Yes: everything human is inevitably (and, to my mind, delightfully) duplicitous. Meaning is always somewhat ambivalent, plural or indeterminate, in every human product – *and a good thing too*, for in struggling to get ourselves out into symbolic expression, we are struggling for therapy. We are trying to synthesize conflicting forces in our own make-up. We are trying to get ourselves together and so become ourselves. Our self-unification is a receding ideal that we must keep pursuing, even though we never fully realize it. And when some unifying symbol does draw us out into coherent expression, we feel very relieved and happy. Our self-expression cheers us up. It is a rather flattering mirror, in which the image is a great deal better-looking than the poor troubled original.

In the book Genesis in the Bible God is pictured as expressing himself in language and thereby building a world into which he puts pleasing images of himself. That is a true myth about *us*;

about how *we* through our self-expression can build our world and recognize in it images of ourselves. Thus for each human being productive work and the struggle for personal wholeness or 'salvation' are one and the same activity. We are trying to become ourselves and to bring forth order out of chaos, both without and within.

So much for 'expressionism'. The new point of view has also been called 'democratic philosophy'. In the past, and for a very long period, philosophies and religious doctrine-systems were much concerned with establishing and confirming hierarchies of value and social control. At every point ordinary people and the world of ordinary life were told that they needed to be and were subject to the authority of something Higher, something normative and standard-setting, something greater in reality, in power, and in value that had the right to govern them. But by 'democratic philosophy' I mean a philosophy that has made a great effort to purge itself of every last trace of such ideas. And I seek to describe the religion of someone who is thoroughly democratic, but who nevertheless goes on wanting to express cosmic yearnings and feelings of love, worship and gratitude; someone who still longs for personal wholeness and redemption, but who cannot find it whilst living under authority.

It should also go without saying that democratic philosophy needs to be generally accessible. It ought not to be written in mystifyingly obscure language, nor in any academic code. It should be clear, as for the most part William James, Nietzsche and the later Wittgenstein are clear. It is if anything even more important that democratic religious writing should be as clear and truthful as it can be made, because if it is *not* clear it will only furnish a pretext for the emergence of yet another class of professional interpreters and controllers of truth.

A third phrase used to describe the new point of view is 'the last philosophy'. By this I mean an idea common to all three of the great modern philosophers, Nietzsche, Heidegger and Wittgenstein: the idea that a very long detour is now over. They mostly see the detour as having lasted some 2,500 years, but

I put it much longer than that. It is the detour through the various forms of belief in something Higher – metaphysics, Platonism, monarchy, sovereignty, or, in a word, the *realism* that objectifies Being and makes an idol of it. The detour is now happily over, and philosophy at last returns into democratic ordinariness, everydayness, the human world, *Dasein*. This everydayness is the place where everything begins and everything ends.

Back in ordinariness, then, the last philosophy returns to something like philosophy's original agenda: how are things with us human beings, how should we live and what can we hope for? The chief gain from the detour is that we have learned that we should begin not with the cosmos, not with matter, not with mind, nor even with the human being, but with *language*. See – here we are now in this sentence, already in language, philosophy's medium. It is the obvious place to begin – so obvious that one marvels how it could have taken so long to see the point. But language (at least, when it runs freely) is supremely democratic and transactional, so that perhaps it was only when philosophy had at last become fully democratic that it became able to see its own medium clearly.

Beginning with language, therefore, we picture it – that is, language – as moving over the interface between subjectivity and the public world. Then we can see the world of subjectivity or selfhood as constructed by interpretation on the inner surface of language, and the public world as constructed on the outer surface.

For an image of how this works, imagine that you have words and empty forms moving rapidly over your eyeball like floating specks. When some sensory content is called up or comes along, and neatly fills a form or activates a word – then, you see something. Looking plus a word equals seeing. Thus the movement of language forms experience and builds the world. A natural language is both a means of expression and a fabulously elegant world-building machine.

As for the question of happiness, notice that when we start

with language in the way I have proposed, there is bound to be a deep affinity and correlation between the state of my subjective feeling on the inner surface of language, and the objective, public state of the world on the outer surface of language. When I am happiest my world is at its most beautiful, and when I am mixed–up and feeling low my world is dreary. Thus we can hope to free ourselves from a number of traditional dualisms, between inner and outer, private and public, spiritual and material and so on. The struggle for personal wholeness and happiness, and the struggle to make the common world a better place, are the same struggle. It's all in the text – and by the way, when we begin with language we understand why in all the great scriptural traditions people have recognized a profound analogy and sympathy between the *microcosm*, the little world of subjectivity that is constructed on the inner surface of the text, and the *macrocosm*, the great objective world that is constructed on the outer surface of the text. The image of a cosmic man crops up, for example, in relation to the figure of Adam in Judaism, in the Perfect Man of Islamic mysticism, in the cosmic Buddha, in the cosmic Christ, and so on. Hence also my own phrase, 'cosmic humanism'.

It is unfortunate that so many modern theologies have tended to assimilate Being to God, and (in pantheism and 'panentheism') the cosmos to God. Being and the cosmos are both of them better seen as finite, temporal and, as one might say, *paired* or correlated with the human self rather than with God. We should see the cosmos as human rather than as divine.

Such very briefly are some of the ideas I have been developing in recent years. I have tried to weave them into what I fancied was a systematically-coherent, but also simple and clear, philosophy and vision of the religious life. But in the past two years or so I have been uncomfortably aware of some loopholes and gaps. After the end of belief in any higher order of being, it is not enough simply to talk negatively about 'non-realism'. A new sort of ontology, or theory of Being, is needed. What is it that is just given, or that gives itself, to us? Without the old belief in substances, how do things hang together; and without any ground in an eternal world, how does the flux of temporal Becoming keep going? How are any identities maintained?

Raising this question, I began to see for the first time that in recent years and without being very clearly aware of it, I have been drawing closer and closer to the later thinking of the great German philosopher Martin Heidegger (1892–1976).[2] It began to seem that I must look more closely at him and start to argue with him. In fact I have been putting him off, and we all know why. Mention Heidegger's name, and many people's noses wrinkle. 'Him? He was a Nazi, wasn't he?' It seems he was, at least in the sense that he joined the Party and then did not resign from it; and it seems too that privately he bitterly regretted having compromised himself so horribly. It is sad that so great a thinker was so badly flawed by cowardice and worldly ambition. Looking for an answer, I can only reply: 'This is the twentieth century. We are all of us compromised.'

But Heidegger remains perhaps the most influential twentieth-century philosopher, and he is certainly the one who has been the most intensively studied by theologians. Living after Nietzsche and being very consciously Nietzsche's successor, Heidegger tried to create a new vision of the human condition and a new way of thinking.

In the older tradition of philosophy from Plato to Kant, philosophy's subject-matter was commonly thought to be 'everything that *must* be true'. Philosophy was oriented towards the realm of Objective Reason and necessary truth, just as religion was oriented towards belief in a metaphysical God. Heidegger, reconstructing thought after the Death of God and the end of metaphysics, attempted to refocus philosophy around human being in time and man's relation to Being.

Theologians, noticing the religious character of much of Heidegger's thought, and (somewhat inaccurately) supposing that he puts Being where traditional religion puts God, have made many attempts to appropriate Heidegger's ideas. They have tried to conscript him into helping them with their project – which, inevitably, turns out to be a relaunch of everything Heidegger was trying to get away from.

What has not yet been attempted is an answer by a theologian to the question, 'What is Being, and what might the religion of Being be like?' One must attempt to extract something clear from Heidegger, but one should not grossly falsify him, as has so often been done. Here, then, using some of his ideas and his vocabulary (but mostly just thinking my own thoughts, as usual), I try to elaborate and state as simply and clearly as possible the outlines of the religion of Being.

One minor but troublesome obstacle needs to be cleared away before we begin. It concerns terminology. Heidegger was very conscious of living after Nietzsche, after the end of metaphysics and in a period haunted by the spectre of nihilism. He felt it necessary to relaunch philosophy. It would be refocussed around the ancient question, 'What is Being?', but doing without the beliefs in an eternal world and in substance. So Heidegger sought to describe a new ontology, *minus* substance and *minus* eternity: *Be-ing*, as the temporal process of forthcoming or eventuating. Be-ing as the unfolding of all things in time. Being as coming *to pass*, so that letting *be* equals letting *go*. Being as pure flitting.

We should start within our own be-ing, for there is nowhere else to start from. Now remove the old belief in a metaphysical core-self or soul, and what is a human life? It is a temporally-extended chain of projects, pursuits, practices and so on, with nothing metaphysical underpinning it and holding it all together. We are 'empty', and Heidegger can speak of the human world, the common world, the world of language, as a 'clearing', the space or the field within which everything that is comes to be and passes away. Our human world just coincides with *the* world, but in a harmless and non-anthropocentric way, because the vision of ourselves and our world as Empty frees us from the will to dominate, allowing us to let beings be and to let the passing show pass away.

As we absorb Heidegger's brand of post-metaphysical philosophy, some curious echoes and affinities come to mind. One side of Heidegger's thinking seems to approach pragmatism, as Richard Rorty has said;[3] but on the other side, Heidegger's thought resembles Buddhist philosophy. Despite the fact that he positions himself so carefully within the Western canon and seldom mentions Asian thought, Heidegger has always been very popular amongst the Chinese and Japanese, and recent studies suggest that he was in fact much influenced both by books and by individuals from East Asia.[4] Indeed, there are places where he equates his notion of Being with the Buddhist idea of Nothingness or Emptiness. Being is the insubstantial and metaphysically-Empty flux of phenomena.

All this helps to explain the curious three-way *rapprochement* out of which this present book arises. In the region of discourse where Buddhists use the word Nothing, Heidegger uses the word Being, and I have for nearly twenty years used the word 'non-realism'. What I call 'realism' (and detest so implacably) is just what Heidegger calls 'Platonism' or 'metaphysics'. The three-way *rapprochement* happened when I realized first that I have long been close to Buddhism, secondly that I have been getting closer to Heidegger, and thirdly that Heidegger himself was well aware of being much closer to Buddhism than most people realize. Like many other moderns, he likes the Buddha's practical, therapeutic and non-metaphysical style.[5] Heidegger understands that Buddhism is not as negative and pessimistic as many nineteenth-century Western writers supposed it to be.

It is a curious feature of philosophy – and especially of the various recent post-metaphysical philosophies – that deep similarities can be almost completely hidden by differences of style, vocabulary and literary personality. It is easy to see that Hume, William James and Nietzsche are very different from each other, but it is much harder to see their deeper resemblances; and something similar is surely true of Wittgenstein and Heidegger. Certainly it has taken me a long time to get clearer about Heidegger and Buddhism. There has been confusion over terminology; and certainly the word 'Being' has acted as a smoke-screen, for me as well as for other and more respectable theologians. Since the mid-1980s I have felt more and more strongly a passionate religious love for pure fleeting contingency. To convey this mood I have tried out many phrases: 'ecstatic immanence', 'glory', 'the mysticism of secondariness' and so forth. But differences of literary personality, vocabulary and style prevented me from realizing that what I was groping after was very much what Heidegger foreshadows as the religion of Being. How slow we are.

This is not an 'academic' study of Heidegger but an experiment in religious thought, and the ideas here presented are presented as mine rather than as Heidegger's. We don't in fact *need* any more 'academic' studies of Heidegger, but we do need more experiments in religious thought. And the direction Heidegger points in is one that deserves to be explored. Not that I always agree with him, as will be seen.

Thanks to Steven Shakespeare and Graham Ward for critical comments, and to Linda Allen again for word-processing.

Cambridge, 1998   DC

1. What is Being?

According to Martin Heidegger, we live in a dark and difficult period dominated by technology and technological thinking, a 'world-midnight', a time when we are too late for God and too early for Being.[1] This is a provoking and fascinating idea, worth pursuing.

Along with a whole series of other German thinkers, Heidegger was inclined to idealize the early Greeks. Just as in Christian theology our first parents in the garden of Eden were held to have enjoyed a natural and perfect communion with God, so Heidegger believed that at the beginning of the Western tradition, Greek thinkers like Heraclitus had been open and responsive to Being. That was the Golden Age. But the whole subsequent history of Western thought has been a Fall-story. With Plato came the Fall into metaphysics, and the beginning of the long forgetting of Being. Instead of living responsively in Being, people turned to seek theoretical knowledge of the realm of beings. Various metaphysical idols were foregrounded one after another, in ways that occluded Being and with ultimately disastrous consequences. In Plato, the Forms; in Aristotle, substance; in Christian thought, God; in early modern thought, the human self; and finally in our own late-modern times, 'the will to will', and the pursuit of unlimited political and technical power just for its own sake. And we, at the end of this sombre history, we wait through the night for Being; we wait for the return of the gods. We wait for the renewal of our long-lost innocence.

What is Being?

From this intriguing and provoking story we gather that Heidegger thinks that in order to reconnect with Being we shall need to recover a forgotten, primordial, pre-theoretical and responsive kind of thinking. This is something that he says we must simply wait for: we cannot regain it by our own efforts. We gather also that Being is not at all the same as God: indeed, for Heidegger the classic Christian-Aristotelian definition of God as 'self-subsistent Being' (*ipsum esse subsistens*) was a very bad mistake. Being should never have been objectified into God in that way, and Heidegger clearly has no wish to see his vocabulary exploited by theologians trying to relaunch God. He points to the ideas of God as Omnipotent and as a craftsman as sources of our own later destructive obsession with technical power harnessed in the service of projects of world-domination. We pictured God as a control-freak, and we became like him. But Being is not a bit like that: rather the opposite, as we shall see in due course.

However, Heidegger's argument seems to require him also to suggest that Being *is* a bit like God after all. He talks as if Being imposes a destiny upon us, Being has a history, Being hides itself and also reveals itself, and as if Being is the central character in a long historical drama of fall and redemption. It seems then that Being has to be both like and unlike God, and Heidegger seems to be caught up in various paradoxes.[2] Thus the God of Christendom was traditionally defined as being *unsurpassably* great and perfect; but Heidegger is claiming that the death of God has already taken place, and God will eventually be replaced by something older and greater than God, something to which we must hope to be restored at some time in the future, if we wait long and patiently enough. So what on earth can Heidegger mean by Being, that makes it such a big *improvement* upon God?

This is not an easy question to answer. Heidegger is a very obscure and difficult writer, who does not tell us really simply and plainly just what he means by Being, what it might be like to live in Being, and how Being might come in time to take the place of God in our lives. And it is not altogether surprising that a man who tells us that we cannot yet know something should be cagey about telling us explicitly just what it is that we cannot yet know. The content of his own message seems to require him to be cryptic in expressing it. And perhaps the same applies to his followers, for Heidegger's numberless commentators and scholars, like Hegel's, have always established their credentials by going native. They prove themselves by mastering his jargon and using it just as he does – which means that they must repeat all his obscurities. They don't make him any clearer, and presumably they cannot do so. Heidegger explained would not be Heidegger: if we really *have* forgotten Being, neither Heidegger nor his commentators are going to be able to explain to us precisely what it is that we have forgotten and cannot know.

All this has been by way of an explanation of the present book. Heidegger is undoubtedly an interesting and important figure. The thesis that we need to try to make a fresh start in philosophy and in religious thought is persuasive, and in some sense or other most people will surely agree that philosophical and religious thinking start when one is shaken with wonder at the mystery of being. But Heidegger's message about Being cannot possibly be right in the form in which he presents it. The matter under discussion is the matter which is of the first importance to every living human person. In so great a matter, the truth simply has to be democratic and universally accessible. It cannot be right that the greatest and most primordial truth of all should be so obscure and élitist that only a tiny clique of specialists (and quite probably not even they) can understand it. And in any case, the idea that in order to be profound you must write badly, though – and for obvious reasons – common in the academic world, is profoundly mistaken.

This book, then, is not written by a Heideggerian, and it does not attempt to add to the existing pile of largely-incomprehensible academic interpretations of Heidegger.[3] I am not concerned to be faithful to Heidegger, and this present essay might best be seen as a reworking or revision of some of his themes and ideas, written half-a-century later and in very different times. But it is a *deviant* reworking.[4] I'm going in the same general direction. Sometimes I cross his path, sometimes I draw upon his vocabulary; but I certainly do not purport to retrace his footsteps precisely. De-via-tion is literally straying off the path, sniffing interestedly at this and that, the way a dog does. That is my procedure. I think that the question of Being is indeed supremely important and interesting, and I do want to state in the clearest and most democratic terms just what Being is, and what a religious thought refocussed around Being might look like. This will require me to diverge a great deal from some of Heidegger's most pessimistic doctrines – and here I mean in particular the doctrines about the history of Being, about forgetfulness of Being, about concealment and so on, that are used to justify the obscurity, the special jargon and the élitism. Instead, I shall do without the ideas of Being's history, forgetting and concealment, and will maintain that although Being is indeed temporal, Being's time is always now, and Being is accessible now. We need to demythologize Heidegger, and to point out that if Being is indeed systematically elusive, it is not so either because it has concealed itself, or because we have forgotten it. Instead I shall argue that the elusiveness of Being is a simple corollary of the nature of language. A natural language is a large, very complex and multi-dimensional system of interrelated meanings, which is highly reflexive – i.e., easily turned back upon itself. The result is what every poet knows – that language is staggeringly good at the world of Meaning, but at no point makes a clear and guaranteed connexion with Being. Language always presupposes Being, skirts it, sees its 'back parts' (here consult Exodus 33.23),[5] but language never quite comprehends Being. It could only comprehend it by grasping its nature, but that is precisely what we shouldn't try to do.[6]

What then *is* Being? Heidegger made, and attaches much importance to, a distinction between Being and beings. By beings he means individual entities, particular existents. Then he says that Being is 'the Being of beings'. But he does not wish us to see Being as merely a universal term, signifying an essence that actual beings have in common, and itself real only in its particular instances. Being gets a capital letter (in the conventional English translations, that is: Heidegger's equivalent move is his adoption of the archaic spelling, *Seyn*, for *Sein*) because it is something like emergence-process, the wonder of the world's moment-by-moment streaming-forth, or outpouring. Being is pure groundless fleeting contingency, already passing away even as it arrives, which is why Being *does* resemble God in allowing us to see only its 'back parts'. Capital-B Being is being that is prior to any determination, pure transience. It cannot be described in language and it cannot be grasped in thought; but it is always presupposed by language, and it sustains language. It gives itself to us, and it emerges within language. We know nothing but the field of view, the field of our own experience. This field is differentiated by language into a field of Be-ing in beings. So Being comes out in our world, the world of language, the only world.

An analogy: an acrobat's performance in a floor exercise always presupposes, and works in a kind of partnership with, the invisible force of gravity. But it is easy for somebody delighted by the performance to overlook gravity and 'forget' the way it always supports the visible show. Similarly, our life, our language and our world-building always presuppose Being; but it is easy to forget Being. Being is always veiled, and not directly in sight.

More of all this as we proceed. It is sufficient here and now for us to note a distinction between those uses of being which can be found also in the plural, beings, and those that are singular only. What Heidegger means by Being is closer to what we mean by saying that some agreement or institution is *in being*: it is thought of as invisibly operative and effective in a continuous present. What is *in being* for *the time being*, or is spoken of as *being the case*, is now continuously operative within a domain, a field or a world. Being, one might say, is that by which beings are and remain in being. It is always off the page, and always coming forward into what is on the page.

There are other strands in the meaning of Being. Pre-Socratic Being, for the early Greeks, was the question of Being, and was overwhelming and abyssal. Heidegger associates the word with a state of disoriented wonder at the world's existence. It is so *in-your-face*. It is a standing or continuous presencing: a *parousia*, as Heidegger says.[7] When it really strikes us, it hits us with the violence of a water-cannon. The people who first philosophized were so transported by the outpouring reckless generosity of all existence that they suddenly saw the entire world of merely-human customs and conventions as ridiculous. They wanted to flee it, and perhaps attempt to remake the human world in the light of the astounding revelation of Being that they had received. So a feeling for Being might make one a cynic like Diogenes; or an ascetic like the Buddha; or even an artist, a poet or a lawgiver.

I experienced the question of Being in this way in 1957. I was having the usual difficulties with the self, and took them along to my philosophy teacher. I complained that the altogether-excessive English vocabulary of the self – psyche, ego, mind, soul, spirit, ghost, etc., etc. – made matters even worse. I was beginning to find that even going to sleep and waking up again were incomprehensible to me. I seemed to be in a state of acute and permanent bewilderment. What *is* the self: what brings it into being and what keeps it in being? What sort of unity does it have? My teacher, a small, calm, composed person, expressed much satisfaction that philosophy was giving me the horrors. He explained that every question in philosophy is far more exciting and terrifying than space travel. '*And* it costs nothing', he added, being a prudent Northerner. Nothing. That didn't help: it made the horrors worse: it has made them lifelong. Philosophy as a subject shares something of Being's own bewildering emptiness and gratuitousness. What is it? – It is everything and nothing.

A third strand in the meaning of Being: Heidegger's discussions use – no doubt deliberately – a good deal of vocabulary which has one set of resonances in philosophy, and another in theology. *Parousia*, just mentioned, is substance in philosophy, but an Advent or even a theophany in theology. *Aletheia*, truth, is literally unconcealment, discovery, un-forgetting, but in theology the same metaphor is employed in the word revelation. One is reminded that as in theology there is a play between hiddenness and revelation, so in philosophy there is a play between what is foregrounded and what is held back. And again, there are similarities and crosslinks between the vocabularies in which theology and philosophy respectively discuss the issues of destiny and freedom.

Heidegger is acutely aware of all these linguistic points. He knows that the vocabulary he is using is highly evocative at several levels. But he may not have been aware of a sexual element in the metaphors that surround his (and later) writing about Being, and they deserve a brief mention here. We begin with the highly masculinist theme of the creation of all things out of nothing, just by the Will of God, the sole Author and Father of all beings. This theme has always been associated with horror at any suggestion that God might have a consort, and indeed that anything female might be divine and creative. However, there are also other idioms in our language that picture all things as coming to birth from the womb of time, the O-Void, the *chora* (= vase or vessel).[8] Out of nothing, a stream of pure contingency pours forth unceasingly, like a well-spring or fountain.

This makes it plain that Heidegger's refocussing of philosophy around Being rather than God involves a certain shift from an almost-exclusively-male metaphoric to a much-more-female metaphoric *especially in relation to the continuous coming-to-be of the creature out of nothing*. In orthodox theology, creation out of nothing is a supreme affirmation of reassuringly dry, solid and upright, or E-rect, male phallic authority. But in Heidegger's philosophy of Being everything pours forth from the female O-Void. Not that Heidegger says so expressly. He is

very willing to admit, and to discuss explicitly, the highly femi-
nine character of remembering, knowing, gathering – in short,
of the new type of thinking that he is trying to teach.[9] But
Heidegger never gets round to discussing explicitly the female-
ness of Being – and the term O-Void is of course my own pun-
ning coinage from the word 'ovoid'. The Nihil is also an *egg*.
Heidegger himself approaches this topic only via his anxiety
about nihilism and how to define it. Stanley Rosen, one of the
very best of all the commentators, himself ends by suggesting
that Heidegger's doctrine of Being falls into rather than over-
comes nihilism.[10] This is the voice of the last-ditch dogmatism
that today uses 'nihilism' and 'relativism' as scare-words. But
why: what is the panic about? Here I plant the suggestion that
the female O-Void is always apt to appear as the Nihil to male
writers, and to arouse in them feelings of dread and metaphysical horror. Heidegger, though normally sensitive to his own
metaphors, does not consider the obvious suggestion that the
forgetting of Being and the enthronement of God the Father in
the whole Western tradition was always linked with, and indeed
powered by, fear of the O-Void and repression of the female
principle. The I has dreaded the O.

I have now said enough to indicate that the field of
metaphors and idioms over which talk of Being may range is
very wide. But as we now begin to deviate from Heidegger and
his commentators, we will quickly narrow down, simplify and
clarify the meaning of Being.

2. Being's time

In Heidegger's use of the term, Being is pre-metaphysical. Being is not a being; that is, Being is not a substance. He is willing to speak of the nothingness of Being, and even (in a rare reference to Buddhist thought) describes Nothing as 'the Eastern word for Being'. He evidently means *sunyata*, the emptiness or insubstantiality or Ground-lessness of everything, which in Japan is described as 'skylike'.[1]

Being is evidently not to be confused with God. Being is not substance, or nature, or form. Nor is Being any sort of force or power. Being is finite. Being is contingent. Being is temporal. More exactly, perhaps, Being is pure flowing, outpouring temporal contingency. It is the well-spring, the Fountain. It is Be(com)ing, a coinage I use by way of pointing back to a place before the arising of the distinction between Being and Becoming. Being as Be(com)ing can't be thought, but it can be surfed in meditation. You should learn to surf it.

Being has no history, just as *sunyata* has no history. It is pure, pre-historical temporality flowing formlessly. When Heidegger talks about 'the history of Being', he must be speaking in a poetical way about the history of Western philosophy, or indeed about human history in general, humanly interpreted. Sometimes he goes further, and anthropomorphizes Being, or ascribes to it some of the attributes of God. But such poetical and theological language is out of place here. Being as such is as formless as the sky. Philosophically-speaking, the history of Being is merely the *human* history of the consequences we have brought upon ourselves by our own forgetfulness of Being. To 'forget Being' is to forget the extreme lightness and fleetingness of everything, and to pursue illusions of absolute reality, power, knowledge and security. The results are ugly. For example, our religion became violent and oppressive, and our world-view too heavy. But this is a painful topic, and I shall not pursue it here.

Being is prior to metaphysics, prior to ideas of 'substance'; and that means that it is even prior to the ordinary Anglo-Saxon commonsense contrast between being and nonbeing. We tend to be, and language tends to be, Aristotelian: we like to operate in terms of a very straightforward binary contrast between something and nothing. So we tend to approach both the question of Being and the question of God in a 'realistic' way: either it is there, or it is not-there. Either a thing is solidly and tangibly present, or it is conspicuously absent. Either you hold that God is an objective being, or you are an 'atheist'. (That at least is what they say to me.) But if this grossly realistic style of thinking is disastrous in relation to God, so it is also even *more* disastrous in relation to Being. Heidegger is arguing that only by slowly learning to think in the new, but also very archaic, non-realist way can we begin to find our way back to Being. He emphasizes very strongly that we are so much the prisoners of the objectifying and instrumental ways of thinking which have become dominant amongst us that it is going to be very difficult indeed to unlearn them. Heidegger seems to be saying that the occlusion and the forgetting of Being which accompanied the development of the Western realistic philosophy of God was so profound that, after the death of God, Being does not and cannot just come flooding back straightaway. Nor can we simply *opt* to remind ourselves of Being and to return into Being. We cannot hope to argue our way home to Being. Being cannot be managed and mastered in thought. As soon as it is coming in, it is already passing away. As soon as you try to get it under control, you've lost it. Indeed, it was precisely the urge to *fix* Being, to objectify it, to master it in thought, that led Plato to make the wrong move that was the beginning of all our troubles. He tried to sever Being from Time. In separating as he did the unchanging and supremely-Real world of the Ideas from the changing and un-real world of experience, Plato introduced an horrendous split between Being and Becoming. He separated Being from its own temporality and, thereby, Be-ing from Itself. He was doing something truly dreadfully wrong, for which we are still paying the penalty. (More about precisely what went wrong, and how the idea of God came to block off our feeling for how to live in Being, in due course.) But two wrongs don't make a right, and the fall into metaphysics cannot be reversed by making a countermove of the same kind but in the opposite direction. No: we must simply wait patiently for Being in the darkness of the world-midnight, attentive and receptive. But Heidegger's account seems to warn us not to try to specify too clearly just what it is that we are waiting for. Like the characters in Samuel Beckett's play (which Heidegger greatly admired, by the way) we are waiting – but we cannot quite know what it is that we wait for, nor how we will recognize it when it comes. Heidegger seems to be saying that Being (poetically speaking) has its own agenda: its own history, its own hour, not under our control.

A paradox now appears. If some such story as this is true, how has Heidegger been able to tell it? How does *he himself* manage to know and to tell us about things that (as he says) we have all of us deeply, deeply forgotten and cannot recover for some time yet? Any statement to the effect that 'We cannot yet know that *p*' becomes paradoxical as soon as a precise value is assigned to *p*. What's hidden from us cannot be described too clearly – what it is, and just where and how it is hidden – without ceasing to be hidden.

Heidegger has two answers to this difficulty. The first is simply to write obscurely. He gives himself airs, adopts the grand manner, and writes in an exalted oracular style. Just what Being is is kept under wraps. Each intriguing but obscure statement about Being is surrounded, not by clearer statements explaining it, but by many further fascinating but equally obscure statements. So Heidegger keeps himself and his teaching a little beyond our grasp. He doesn't become quite explicit enough for the paradoxes to show.

Heidegger's second recourse is to appeal to the history of Western philosophy, which can show us at least something of what went wrong, and what we lost. The key thought here (both for him and for Derrida, I suspect) is that the standard metaphysical theism under which we lived for so long was overwhelmingly violent.[2] Being, made timeless and then objectified, came to be seen as creating the world of Becoming by a pure act of will. We lived with an infinite, immutable, inscrutable Will, unknowable and wholly Other, but less than a whisker away from us, and determining, knowing and judging everything. In retrospect, it is now impossible to imagine how human beings were able to endure such extraordinary terrorism.[3] Does anybody else alive remember how utterly terrible it was, I wonder? But its effect was to numb our senses, our feelings, and indeed our reason. After the violence of God, Being is too mild and gentle for us to be able to receive it – yet, at least. We are like hyperactive, stressed-out people who know we need to relax, but who find it impossible to do so; we are like disgusting old roués, too coarsened to be able to recapture the delicate ardour of first love; we are like people who cannot hear the music of the spheres because it is too murmurous, sweet and constant. To live in Being again we must wait, and calm down. Thus the history of philosophy may help us to understand how we got to our present position, and it may encourage us to hope that after we have recovered from the trauma of the death of God, if we wait patiently, spiritual rejuvenation may yet come to us.

Imagine a person coming out of the certainties of Islam into liberal democracy. Such a person might at first feel orphaned, rudderless in a world of relativities, disoriented and spiritually distressed. But gradually she comes to see that liberal democracy is after all not a weaker but a much *stronger* political system than absolute monarchy, that a morality based only on a slowly-shifting human conversational consensus is actually a far *better* morality than a repressive morality of 'absolutes', and that a purely time-bound spirituality of the body, the emotions and open-ended Becoming is better than a spirituality in which we seek ourselves to become as rigid and vacant as Eternity. Perhaps the changeover from God to Being will involve some such slow process of personal and spiritual re-education. After a bad start, gradually things will come to look better and better.

Now we begin consciously to diverge from Heidegger by saying that, fifty years later, it is no longer necessary to be obscure, nor to picture ourselves as being the captives of our own historical period. We avoid the paradox and the need for obscurity that have so badly affected his writing by saying simply that the time for Being is now. It is always the time of Being. Temporality is Being's *modus vivendi*, its manner of Be-ing. Being is always with us, and in us. It pours out change unchangingly, silently, effortlessly. Being is always Be-ing. The Fountain is never switched off.[4] Heidegger, although he is critical of theology, still keeps a sort of theology of history, according to which what is spiritually possible for us is circumscribed by the dispensation, or stage in the great historical drama, in which we are presently living; and although he is no Hegelian he still tells a long story about the history of exclusively-Western philosophy which, again, suggests that the way we think is constrained by the general character of the particular time within which we think. In a word, Heidegger is an historicist, and an all-Western historicist to boot. He allows himself to seem Eurocentric, at just the moment when after nearly 500 years the epoch of European cultural world-leadership was finally ending. Too much of the time, he writes as if he thinks that philosophy just is Western philosophy, that the history of philosophy just is the history of Western philosophy, and indeed that the story of Western philosophy is some kind of *cosmic* drama in which we are all of us caught up, involuntarily. But now, fifty years on, his Eurocentrism looks very dated. Globalization has made us citizens of the world, and we need no longer see ourselves as confined to one local tradition only.

I am suggesting, then, that we need not be bound either by Heidegger's obscurity or by his pessimism. We just do not have to suppose that the West is going down like the *Titanic*, and taking us with it. Study of the history of Buddhist philosophy, and especially of such great figures as Nagarjuna, Candrakirti and Dōgen, can help us to escape from the feeling that we have been made the prisoners of our own Western history.[5] To escape, all we have to do is to step into another history. It is easy, dead easy – perhaps because the dominance of fiction amongst literary forms has made it so much easier for us than it was for our ancestors to adopt and try out another vision of the world. Western philosophy may indeed have forgotten Being, but the Eastern history is different, and it is certainly arguable that the very thing that Heidegger waits patiently for is actually delivered in Madhyamika teaching – as he was surely himself told by his Japanese interlocutors. And if he knew that the whole notion of a Western Canon is dead, why was he still so keen to arrange for himself a place in it?

Why then should we not now say clearly what Being is, and what it is to live in Being? Nothing prohibits us from doing so *now*. Being does not hide or withhold itself. It pours out into history, but it has itself no history. Certainly, it is radically temporal, but its way of changing all the time does not change. It emerges, e-ventuates, continuously. It always pours out, silently, effortlessly coming forth into itself, Be(com)ing into being. As all the time it quietly pours out and passes away, it continuously and evenly replaces itself, like a fountain that recycles its own waters.

In H.G. Wells' novel, the Invisible Man could come out in public only when culturally wrapped, dressed in clothes. Naked, he could not be seen. So Being likewise comes out clothed in language and in the world of language – as now, in this sentence. And because Being is *always* language-clad in the way it is in these running sentences you now peruse, I can write Being in language clearly and without paradox. (At least, I can in principle do so: in practice it is not so easy.) If Being is always language-mediated as now, then these sentences about it are not, cannot be, entirely incongruent with it. The medium, which is sentences about Being, is in full accord with the message about life in Being, as we shall see. (Briefly, as we live in language, Being comes forth in language. In language, we express ourselves and form our world. Being gives itself to us all the time as our own human being, and as our language-formed human world. Being is *mitmenschlich*, with us, for us. It is not at all alien or strange.)

It should be clear by now that this present essay is not intended to be a book about Heidegger; and I make no pretensions whatever to be an interpreter of Heidegger. If you want the 'scholars', go to them, and good luck to you. I am thinking *after* Heidegger, sometimes *with* him, and sometimes *against* him. His name, and indeed the very *word* 'Being', have here the same sort of function as an establishing shot in cinematic narrative. And that's all. Too much should not be made of any particular terms or proper names. We might, for example, have preferred to use throughout the text the term of art 'Be(com)ing', or alternatively the phrase that I have preferred elsewhere, 'the Fountain'. It belongs roughly where Nietzsche puts the eternal return, invoking a flux of pure contingency that pours out and passes away so evenly and quickly that it eternally brings itself back again. The Fountain is self-renewing pure empty contingency, healing and reposeful, that simply, very *simply*, does not need any absolute or metaphysical Ground. One can be completely happy with it just as it is. It is a symbol of the post-metaphysical religious object: think of the way that thought, language and natural energies, all of them, *stream* forth. In meditation, we surf that streaming-forth.[6]

Here, instead of beginning with the Fountain, we've begun with Being, because of Heidegger's attractive suggestion that as our religious psychology recovers from the extreme and crippling violence of the old metaphysical belief in God we may find ourselves easing, and becoming able to receive and appreciate a new and altogether milder object, Being.

Being is so easy, going.

3. Be(com)ing

To get into Being, to attune ourselves to Being, to learn to respond to Being, we need to free ourselves – which in effect means, we need to free our *language* – from a series of distinctions that together have had the effect of alienating us from Being, and even from Being's forthcoming within ourselves.

Of these distinctions, the most important is that between Being and Becoming. Undoing the distinction, we should simply elide the two words together: Be(com)ing. 'Being' is a present participle. Being *is* its own becoming, its own continual self-replacement as it slips into being and slips away.

In talking of Being as slipping into being I am conscious of being paradoxical, and with a purpose. The point is that when we speak of Being, there is always something there already, something presupposed, something that seems to precede language and cannot quite be captured in language. Being is prior to any determination by language: as soon as it has come out into expression in language, it has slipped away. Derrida calls it transcendental, using the word 'transcendental', I think, in the old medieval sense rather than in Kant's way. Language always presupposes it, but cannot quite succeed in fixing it and making it clear. Heidegger in a well-known essay makes the point by writing B~~ei~~ng – crossed-out but still legible, 'under erasure'.[1]

Nobody nowadays is likely to copy Heidegger's device of writing B~~ei~~ng under erasure. But there is a better way of making his point about the elusiveness of Be-ing. It is this: language is all about *meanings*. It is a wonderfully flexible medium, easily

26

turned back upon itself so that it can be used to talk about itself. We do this, for example, with the help of the well-known use/mention distinction: a word that is *mentioned* is in effect singled out and put in quotes so that it can be talked about. In talking about it, we may make *use* of the same word; but we feel no difficulty at all about this. Language is very good at talking about itself; talking, that is, about the uses and meanings of words. So good is it, indeed, that Heidegger began his late essay 'The Way to Language' (1959) by quoting a line from Novalis to the effect that language is *only* about itself.[2] But language is very bad at jumping clear of itself in order to grapple with extra-linguistic *existence*. How can it? A symbol-system is a system of meanings: how could you build into it, or deliver within it, a clear explanation of how there gets to be something to which it has application? Nothing within, for example, simple arithmetic says or can say that there *has* to be anything to which it applies.

The difficulty here has long been familiar to philosophers and theologians in the standard criticism of Anselm's proof of the existence of God. This proof is usually called 'The Ontological Argument' – Kant's misnomer. The true crux of the matter is that Anselm is trying to prove that in one unique case a meaning is such that it guarantees actual being. But if we agree with the philosophers' consensus that Anselm fails in the special case, then *a fortiori* we must acknowledge that language, as a system of inter-related meanings, cannot anywhere internally guarantee its own hookup to real extra-linguistic existence. As the long debate about Anselm's proof has shown, the link between language and nonlanguage cannot itself be demonstrated within language. And if therefore Anselm's proof is dead, realism generally is dead; and we thus understand how and why it is that the very same feature of language that makes it so good at talking about Meaning also entails that it never quite masters Being.

Now consider the consequences. Because language itself is so heavily tilted away from Being and towards Meaning, philosophical writing will always tend to resolve questions about Being into questions about Meaning. If you are Plato, you will end up turning being into essence, and the Real World into an order of intelligible essences – a dictionary in the sky. If you are a modern linguistically-aware person, you are bound to find yourself in the end resolving the individual entity into a cluster of descriptions. Language simply cannot take you any further than that. It does not in fact jump beyond itself to comprehend the thing-in-itself. It cannot. So the nature of language ensures that all great philosophical traditions, Eastern and Western, will tend to develop towards idealism and then topple over into scepticism, or nihilism, or Wittgensteinian quietism. Similarly, mathematical physics tends to end up worrying that it has forgotten Being. Its theories become more and more refined, and somehow less and less able to tell us what it is for there to be something to which they apply. If metaphysics cannot fix Being, nor can physics either. Similarly, it is perhaps because language is so tilted towards Meaning and away from Being that someone like me who has given his whole life to philosophy and to theology ends up darkly suspecting that poetry, myth and fiction are far superior as literary forms, because they run so much more closely with and along the grain of language. All those millennia of civilization – and I end up less good than the humblest tribesman relating a myth? It's galling.

Being then is systematically elusive. Language always presupposes it but can never get hold of it. One should put it under erasure, B̶e̶i̶n̶g̶; or one should instead say simply that Being is its own Becoming; it continually slips into itself and slips away. It is pure contingency, the underlying unmasterable givenness or gratuitousness – or graciousness – of everything, and we should not ask either where it comes *from* or where it is going *to*. With people, to be born is not to come from somewhere, and to die is not to go away to somewhere else; and so it is with Being. We should not be misled by popular euphemisms. The world of language and the world of life are simply coextensive. Language cannot get hold of regions that are *ex hypothesi* prior to it, or outside it. Nor should we follow those theologians who try to put back the clock and convert Being back into the old meta-physical God: that is a very bad misuse of Heidegger, and an even worse misreading of our present condition. In particular, we should not try in any way to revive talk of eternal being, out-side of and prior to time. Nothing is eternal. Being *is* temporal forthcoming, and there is no real being apart from temporality. To pun: Being comes just in time. In which case, the old dis-tinction was radically wrong. It set up two sharply-contrasted worlds, the world of Becoming and the world of Being. The world of Becoming was the visible world of ordinary human experience, the human life-world. It was a world of continually-changing appearances, the 'passing show' of transient pheno-mena, and was regarded therefore as unreal. By contrast, real Being was set up as eternal Being, self-subsistent, luminously intelligible and unchanging. It was located not in this world but in a higher and invisible world – the world of eternal truth that philosophers contemplated, the heavenly world of religion, or (its last incarnation) the Kantian world of thought, the world of pure Reason.

So the everyday world, the world of time and Becoming, was sharply contrasted with the world of eternal Being. And when these ideas are taken up into theology, the results are not happy. If real Being is eternal Being, then it must be unknowable by us who live in the realm of Becoming; and conversely, if we ask just *how* the world of Becoming issues from its absolute Ground in eternal Being, the answer given us is that the whole realm of Becoming depends only upon the simple fiat ('Let it be so') of an omnipotent and inscrutable Will. That is it: no further explanation is available. In effect, we are told that there *is* an explanation, but it is not for us. So the classical metaphysical theism involved, and for believers still involves, a condition of extreme alienation from Being. God is infinitely different, wholly Other than us. We cannot call upon God to explain his decrees.

To this objection the classical Islamic and Christian theologians replied that the unknowable Creator has nonetheless graciously planted analogies both of himself and of the God/World, Being/Becoming distinction all over the created order. But if the Being/Becoming distinction is in itself a very bad thing, we may well wonder whether to be glad or sorry that the human world is so shot through with analogies of it. Will they not have the effect of constantly reminding us that our human condition is tragically and incurably divided – or perhaps rather, *making* it so?

Certainly the oppositions are numerous and varied. Religion dramatized and elaborated the contrast between the two orders to such a degree that it came to pervade our whole culture – i.e., all our language. Think, for example, of the wide-ranging influence of the contrasts between principle and practice, the pure and the applied, reason and sense, the head and the heart, the absolute and the relative, freedom and necessity, form and content, substance and process, and the spiritual and the material. All over the culture and in almost every area of life we are busy making the same sort of contrast, between that which has a short-term superficial appeal to the senses and the emotions, and that which is solid, long-term, cerebral, masculine, authoritative and demanding.

How is it possible, and why is it desirable, to attempt to undo binary ways of thinking and linguistic oppositions that are so numerous and so deeply-entrenched?

The answer is that the intelligible world, the world of values and of meanings, the world of our ideal culture, the world of philosophy, can no longer be thought of as a timelessly-real world of eternal Being. Everything is temporal; the former absolutes, certainties and timeless verities have already disappeared from the world. There are none of them left: since about the time of Hegel, the whole eternal world has melted away. In the traditional cultures of the past the ideal order was indeed portrayed as a world of unchangingly authoritative and objective realities. Tradition was itself an unchanging 'absolute'. But nowadays the entire ideal order has been demythologized simply into *language*. In the stock Heideggerian phrases, 'language is the house of Being' and 'Man is the shepherd of Being'; and language is now understood to be not a fixed and stable system of meanings, but something that is fluid, shifting and changing all the time. Even as we use it, we are continually changing it. The effect of this is that the former eternal world has now become simply a collective, evolving human social construction. It is culture. This shows us why it is that the worlds of Being and Becoming have now become one and the same, for Being's own coming forth into everyday being is identical with its formation by language. Being's manifestation, its coming to light, coincides with its arrival clothed in language. *Genesis*, the world's coming into Being, is happening all the time in us and through us. But there is no tradition-fixed objective Cosmos any more. There is no ready-made world out there. The world we build around ourselves is now seen to be changing and developing along with us who are building it. It is our own 'objectivity', our expression.

The new world-view that I'm trying to describe involves a very great simplification. Indeed, what makes the new point of view, and the reality of Being, so hard to grasp is not its abstruseness and difficulty, but its extreme closeness and simplicity. It is *blindingly* obvious.

In the past it was widely thought that the distinguishing characteristic of the truths of philosophy was the fact that they were universal and *necessary* truths. Philosophy was concerned with everything that *must* be so, and to work it all out involved much training and disciplined use of one's powers of reasoning. Correspondingly, the great and saving truths of religion were more than just hard to reason out. They were altogether *above* reason. We couldn't come at them by our own unaided efforts, and had to believe them on the authority of a duly-accredited proponent who put them to us.

Here, I am proposing a third and very different view. The truth about Being is hard to attend to and hard to appreciate (i.e., appraise) properly, not because it either stretches or transcends our faculties, but merely because it is so close and so obvious. The great truths of philosophy, religion and ethics – and I mean here simply the truths in those areas that matter the most to every human person – are right under our noses. They are so utterly platitudinous and democratic that all you have to do in order to discover them is simply to empty your head of all the historically-accumulated rubbish that clogs it, sit back patiently, and wait quietly for them all to appear and make themselves known. 'Just sit', advises Dōgen correctly, and he compares the meditator with somebody who sits very still in a forest, until all the animals come out. The simile is a good one. The animals are there already and we all know their names, but most of us have never got around to sitting still for long enough to give them time to come out and show themselves to us. So it is with philosophical and religious truth. We have heard of it, but we are always too *busy* for it. We haven't given it a chance to appear to us personally.

But we know that that is how it is with human beings. As in the Edgar Allen Poe story about the Purloined Letter, the nearest and most obvious thing is always the hardest to see. When someone giving us directions declares in a confident tone that 'You can't miss it', we know for sure that we will very soon be doing just that.

The outstanding example of something very close and important that we just cannot see is the world of symbolic or linguistic meaning. Most people still seem to have no notion of its existence. We have during the twentieth century very gradually become aware of it, as a number of different systems of thought have converged: the comparative study of religions and mythologies, the dynamic depth-psychologies of Freud, Jung and their followers, and then more recently structuralism and post-structuralism. In their varied ways all these rich and complex movements were pioneering attempts to explore the logic and the dynamics of the world of myth, the world of symbolic meaning, the world of language – a world that every one of us is already immersed in all the time, yet a world that it remains amazingly difficult for us to get a clear view of. We have been in it since our early childhood. Indeed, the first books that are read to young children are largely *about* it. In the beginning is the Word. It is our natural habitat, but we just cannot see it.

So it is with Being. Being is obvious. Being is as close as can be, 'Nearer to us than breathing, closer than hands and feet'. Being surely cannot be a problem to us: we are all of us in Being already. What is more, Being is, as it were, our partner. It works with us. There are no ultimate mysteries, because there is no great and superhuman mind in which are stored great Truths that are above us and beyond our comprehension. There is nothing that is incomprehensible by us because it is just willed, without reason. Nothing is hidden. There are no mysteries. Everything is just a gift, in the popular sense of 'gift' – i.e., *dead easy*, as easy as falling off a log. Once we understand the *point* of the *humanity* of all language, all meaning, all truth, and see that Being itself is with, for and in *us*, is *mitmenschlich*, then we see that there isn't and cannot be anything radically uncanny or unfamiliar to us. All things are ours: Being itself is ours. We should experience Being as so easy and familiar that it liberates us from all anxiety, fear and *belief*. Belief is needed only where there is some measure of alienation. But Being is not far away from us. It couldn't be closer. Yet how are we ever going to learn the trick of waiting upon Being, attending to it?

This is what one might call an experimental question, and I will describe Five Ways that seem to work – for this rather backward and primitive Westerner, at least. Remember that we are not trying to attend to *timeless* Being, but simply to *temporal* Be(com)ing. That is why we begin with two forms of Moving-Edge Meditation, a form of meditation in which we try to concentrate our attention upon watching the unfolding of the Now-moment, Dōgen's *Nikon* and Meister Eckhart's *Nu*. We are watching time be-ing. We are not attempting to abstract away either from sensuousness or from contingency. On the contrary, most of us need to become *more* sensuous, not less; our present problem is rather that in our culturally-very-rich epoch we all of us bring to experience such a huge quantity of theory, interpretations and expectations from the past, and hopes and fears for the future. We are so very busy interpreting experience that we have *no time for time*. We jump to conclusions so quickly – and, no doubt, usually correctly – that we get ahead of ourselves. We fail to allow ourselves to slow down and attend upon the forthcoming of Be(com)ing.

So that is what we should try to do. It is best quietly to watch some irregular natural motion – an insect, leaves in the wind, a dog, a person sleeping or walking in the distance. The motion will act as a memento, a reminder of time and a focus. Watch the front edge of the wheel, the foot, the wave, the wing. Watch time pass. Watch Becoming. Attend to the *Nu*, with as narrow a bandwidth or 'specious present' as possible. Try to sit completely still on the leading edge of Now. If you can do it, it is ravishing, perhaps because it empties out the self. One feels snatched away, transported. *And* it costs nothing. In a way that is somehow prior to language and uncapturable in language, we learn that Being, motion and time are all the same. At least, one cannot tell them apart. There is only Be-ing. Being supports the Empty self, somewhat as an uprushing jet of air or water may support a ping-pong ball that rests upon it. But in this form of meditation, one tries not to verbalize but only to attend. The relation to Being is tacit, and not articulate: in that respect at least Moving-Edge Meditation does resemble traditional contemplative prayer.

That is the *extravertive* version of moving-edge meditation. One tries to surf the Moment, the *Nu*, and lets Being be. One tries to keep in time with Time. In step. The *introvertive* version (described in *The Last Philosophy*, chapter 3) attempts to watch the coming-forth of Be(com)ing as language in one's own subjectivity while lying awake at night thinking. In the dark, quiet and relaxed, we can faintly hear the rhythmic surgings of our own physiology. Feelings, looking for forms in which to express themselves, run into and activate words. Trains of thought, sentences, begin to move – and a miniature cosmogony has been enacted in one's own head as language moves over the primal Chaos. The opening verses of Genesis have taken place within our subjectivity as we lay in the dark. When biological affect has run into and activated a verbal form, thought stirred, language began to move, *and there was light!* That, *that* is Be(com)ing, the coming forth from Chaos of a lit-up and language-formed world. And it all happens in your own head every night. It is astounding. Just watch it!

The third and fourth ways involve making a habit of reflecting upon *metaphors* that help to make Be-ing more accessible and thinkable. Our thinking may be so dominated by old metaphors (ground, foundation, a chain running back into a fixed point of anchorage, etc.) that the new way of thinking about Being is difficult to assimilate. New and friendly metaphors can help us to accustom ourselves to new assumptions and new ways of thinking.

First, *the Fountain*, and with it perhaps the Torus. We should see the whole of reality as like a great fountain that continuously recycles its own waters. From a distance, a fountain or a waterfall may appear motionless, silvery and almost solid; but as we draw near and examine the fountain more closely we see that it contains nothing substantial or self-identical at all. It is composed of nothing but a rush of pure formless contingency, pouring out and scattering. It is wholly and perpetually utterly fleeting. But why should this state of things ever have seemed to be in any way wrong or unsatisfactory? A fountain is after all a universally-loved symbol of life, refreshment, healing and repose. Furthermore, one might imagine a cosmological fountain, a cyclical Universe in which all the energy dissipated in the expansion-phase is recovered in the contraction-phase. Now we suppose that what philosophers call the 'B-theory' of time is true.[3] Then all times are equally real, time is a closed circle, and the whole Torus is in effect 'self-existent' and sempiternal. Every bit of reality is insubstantial and fleeting, but it all adds up to a totality that just is, without needing to be grounded in an eternal order of Being. In fact, meditating upon and developing the Fountain-metaphor can gradually cure us of the feeling that we need to distinguish between time and eternity, Becoming and Being. And when we have reached that point, we may see that we are completely happy with Be(com)ing. It is at once and undividedly perpetual *and* fleeting, in motion *and* still, contingent *and* self-existent, and so on. It precedes and makes unnecessary the old distinctions. In fact, it really is an improvement upon the old God. It is prior to God, because it is prior to the old distinction between God and the creature, and it makes that distinction unnecessary.

The second metaphor for consideration is *cinematic*. It invites us to see the successive states of the world as succeeding each other like the successive frames of a cine-film, but very much more rapidly. In the old Indian thought a *ksana* was a sixty-fifth of a second, and in Mahayana Buddhist philosophy it came to be said that a whole cycle of birth-and-death happens in every moment of time. Dōgen goes still further in accelerating the furiously-rapid spinning of the Wheel of Time, by assuring us that there are 6.4 billion *ksanas* in every twenty-four hours (*Shobo-genzo,* fascicle *Hotsu Bodai-shin*).[4] We transmigrate continuously, he says, and he actually maintains that when we become aware of the featherlight, high-speed flux of all Being the world becomes beautiful – 'the earth becomes gold, and the ocean nectar' – and we are awakened to the Bodhi-mind: which means that we long to see all sentient beings achieve enlightenment. 'Even soil, sand, rocks and pebbles manifest the Bodhi-mind, as do ocean-spray, bubbles and flames.'[5] Fully to recognize universal high-speed transience, and in that recognition to love one's fellow-being – that, that, says Dōgen, is salvation:

> We should not forget even for a moment that our life is in a constant state of birth and decay. If, constantly keeping this in mind, we vow to help others cross over to the other shore before doing so ourselves, eternal life immediately appears before us.[6]

In the West the suggestion that all things are very insubstantial and transient, and *therefore* very beautiful, is commonly considered not a religious but a pagan sentiment: *sunt lachrimae rerum et mentem mortalia tangunt* (There are tears shed for things, and mortality touches the heart: *Aeneid* i, 462). But one may reply that in some contexts, as when we put flowers on a grave, symbols of life's transience are not felt to be at all irreligious. And is it not the case that we love with a peculiarly intense and unselfish passion those things that are too ephemeral to be possessed? We cannot grab such things, and *our heart goes out* to them. However, extreme emphasis upon the temporality of all Be-ing in Heidegger's manner and upon the velocity-of-light speed of transience in Dōgen's manner has led to accusations of nihilism. Nietzsche describes Buddhism as 'passive nihilism', and the West has still not entirely shaken off the old assumption that Buddhism is pessimistic and life-denying.

In reply, I say that it is a mistake to make a bogey of something called 'nihilism'. What is it? What's wrong with it? What's its antonym, anyway? Let us forget the bogey, and simply give up the idea that there can be any non-temporal thought, or linguistic meaning, or matter, or being. When we are able to say a wholehearted Yes to transience, we become able to experience the self-presenting of Be(com)ing, Be-ing's gift of itself just in time.

The fifth and final way to become more aware of and more responsive to Being as Be(com)ing is by getting into the habit of noticing the rich and altogether wonderful vocabulary that we have for the coming forth of Being *in language*. The world of language is the world of *broad* daylight, the open, the common world, and Be-ing is coming forth into the light of the common world, much as a baby, when it is brought forth, is said to have 'come into the world' out of the darkness of the womb, the O-void.

Being is coming forth, e-ventuating, coming to expression, coming to birth, coming to light, coming out into the open, coming into the world, coming *clean* (now I think of it). Being is happening, and perhaps you have noticed the happy connections between hap and happiness, fortune and fortuity. As well as the theological-bureaucratic tradition in our culture which regards the best world as a world in which everything is determined, foreordained, destined, tightly managed and controlled, and nothing is left to chance, we also have a wise popular tradition that praises *fors* and hap, chance and luck, and regards pure contingency as a sort of blessing. If everything is purely contingent, we don't need to get involved with looking for someone or something to blame. Not God, not my neighbour, not myself. Things just happen. Just happen, just in time. Just. Only just.

Being is happening, Being energizes language, comes to manifold and varied expression in language: and Being's coming into expression in language through us is our world. The world.

4. Hap-hap-happy

Being is finite. Being is contingent: that is, it is not necessitated, but just happens, all the time. Being is pure unformed Becoming, slipping into itself and slipping away, vanishing as it appears. It is gratuitous, even gracious; but it is not any thing. Whether it takes form and becomes the be-ing of a concrete existent being depends upon the availability of linguistic and other symbolic forms for it to run into, fill and activate. 'In itself', Being is prior to form or any determination. It so-to-say partners or collaborates with us humans in the building of our many and varied worlds. 'In itself', it is not any sort of legislator or Cosmocrator.

Being is thus quite different from God, and might indeed be seen as God's Other. For God is pure Form, pure legislative and controlling Will: God is the supreme determiner, whereas Being is gentle, plastic, continually-emergent receptivity to Form. God presides over and rules just one world that is at every point wholly subject to his Will, whereas Being is amoeboid. It can and does take many forms or none; it is open to endless meta-morphosis. Monotheists tend to see divinity always in terms of Power, but Being is divinely plastic, polymorphous and irides-cent.

In the epoch of God, there is a single fully-determinate created world, a cosmos that is governed from its ground in the prior world of linguistic meaning, the symbolic order, a realm which is seen as being highly organized, structured, unified. It is the Mind of God, who is the master of all meaning. So: a single Cosmos, the expression of a single absolute governing Mind.

In the epoch of Being, the world of meaning is multi-dimensional, plural and subject to endless magical transformations – and so therefore is also the empirical world.

For the epoch of God, an appropriate literary genre might be Leo Tolstoy's clear-cut moral realism. For the epoch of Being, Salman Rushdie's magical realism is more fitting.

There is one perhaps-decisive piece of evidence that the world-epoch ruled by God has recently come to an end, and the epoch of Being has begun. It is this: in the last generation or so, people at large have come clearly to recognize that a world in which everything is contingent, mere happenstance, is much to be preferred to the old moralistic world-order, in which every event was very strictly foreordained and ordered towards the eventual realization of a great moral design. People are finding that they no longer wish for a One-Truth law-and-order universe with everything under close divine control, in the Calvinist manner; they are finding that they prefer a picaresque disorderly world of many truths, ups and downs, and caprices of fortune. We no more wish to inhabit a theocratic *universe* than a theocratic *society*. As for the old very severe moralism – it now looks *im*moral.

Suppose that you are going to visit a rather young friend who has recently been diagnosed as terminally ill. What will you say? In the age of God nothing was accidental, and everything had a moral purpose. A moral reason could always be given why everything that was so, was so. This sickness, the visitor was instructed to say, was 'certainly God's visitation', 'whether it be to try your patience, for the example of others', or alternatively, 'to correct and amend in you whatsoever doth offend the eyes of your heavenly Father'. So you must 'repent you of your sins, and bear your sickness patiently', rendering unto God 'humble thanks for his fatherly visitation'.

Such was the classical theist's response to another's grave

illness, as laid down in the *Book of Common Prayer* (1662). In a subsequent period this seemed too harsh, and something called 'the problem of evil' became prominent instead. Why does a loving God allow innocent, decent folk to suffer so extremely, through natural disasters, painful illnesses and unavenged criminal injustices? In a world supposedly governed by a loving God, innocent suffering presented an agonizing religious problem, of which one was acutely aware when visiting a young person's deathbed.

The age of the problem of evil lasted from about 1690 to 1970, from Newton to chaos theory and from William King to John Hick, or thereabouts.[1] Nowadays, when we hear that a friend has been the victim of a serious accident or is terminally ill, we say simply 'How dreadful! What rotten luck'. To our surprise, we suddenly notice that we have quite lost the old urgent need to find a moral reason, some possibility of moral gain, or alternatively someone or something to be *blamed*. And we are glad to be relieved of a burden. We do not want to go back to the old ways of thinking. We do not want to regard misfortunes as punishments. We don't want to be passing moral judgement upon everyone and everything, all the time. We do not want any more to see the world as a classroom ruled by a sharp-eyed, super-efficient and moralistic Schoolteacher who always knows precisely what degree of merit or demerit currently attaches to each and every pupil in the class. In fact we find that mere hap is happier than a moral providence ever was.

It is difficult to imagine the scale of the cosmological revolution that we have quite recently gone through. It reaches back further and is wider in its implications even than the story of the birth and death of God. Briefly, from Upper Palaeolithic times until the nineteenth century or so and in almost every culture, if you suffered some affliction you could expect your local religious system to offer you a narrative moral explanation of *why* you were suffering, and professional advice as to the appropriate remedy. At one time or another, most people wanted to know: 'Why this evil? And what am I do to about it?'

– and answers were provided. You had incurred pollution, the spirits were offended, you had sinned, a neighbour was working magic against you; and whatever the explanation, a ritual therapy or form of counteraction was available.

Christian theology also stood in this same ancient tradition, providing both short-term personal and long-term communal accounts of the divine purpose for human life. God would triumph in the end, and evil would be overcome. In the meanwhile, there was repentance and absolution; there were the Sacraments. And throughout the entire ten millennia and more, the presumption generally held that events – and above all, misfortunes – are never just random. *Every event could be seen as being part of a story* about a larger purpose, good or evil. Even as recently as the 1960s conservative-minded persons were still saying that they simply could not accept the thought that an innocent person's sudden death might be just an unlucky accident that 'means nothing'. If that were ever true, C.S. Lewis once said, 'reality at its very root would be meaningless to us'. He felt real horror at the thought of pure hap, with no 'explanation', no 'meaning' and no 'good coming out of it'.

I read all Lewis's books, met and talked with him, and in the 1950s felt exactly as he did. But today we have almost all of us changed utterly. After a natural or a personal disaster, we no longer feel the old urgent need to cry out: 'How can a good God allow such a thing to happen?' People are deeply glad to find themselves liberated from all the old acute religious distress, the intellectual dishonesty and the foolish stock answers. A friend, a Christian minister, wrote to me after his much-loved wife's premature death from cancer to say what a relief it had been to be able to think of her illness as a mere statistical misfortune. Nobody was to be blamed, and nobody was being punished. Meaninglessness is profoundly liberating, and a great comfort. We should be grateful for it. Mischance is innocent, whereas providentially pre-planned suffering is horrible and terrifying. My friend didn't have to struggle to work out what good moral reason God might have had for afflicting his wife. He had been freed simply to love and care for her to the end, as anyone else nowadays would wish to do.

We have, then, lived through a major revolution in world-view. By an interesting paradox, in the great days of theology when people knew next to nothing about how the world goes, they were fully convinced that everything was intelligible and under control, and served a wise moral purpose. They were very confident, because they were so ignorant. Nowadays the vast expansion of our knowledge has served chiefly to persuade us gradually to become accustomed to the ideas of probability and chance. The world is neutral. We humans are the only ones who try to impose a moral order upon our life, and we are never wholly successful in our attempts. On any view, there remains a large element of just hap in life: and what is remarkable is that we find ourselves so unexpectedly happy about it. We are not troubled by the thought that the new vision is of a world and a life become absurd, or 'utterly meaningless'. On the contrary, as I have suggested, Being is not alien. It is gentle, contingent, slipping into itself and slipping away, gratuitous in a way that is even *gracious*, partnering us in our world-building. We can, we should, say a religious Yes to Being, living in Being happy-go-lucky. What Lewis called meaninglessness, I now call divine, and have learnt to love it. Innocent contingency.

We have lived through a revolution. Yet now that we are all through it, we can see that our new readiness to say Yes to life, even though life is by our own former standards now seen to be chaotic, random and 'meaningless', is not so new after all. It is abundantly anticipated in common speech, in dozens of idioms and etymological connections that we've always been familiar with. It is as if the speech of ordinary people was always much wiser and craftier than our official creeds and philosophies: as if ordinary people always reckoned that life is a great blessing even though they knew perfectly well that it is disorderly and random, with no antecedently-inbuilt Plan or moral order or meaning whatsoever. Once again, truth has always been more democratic than we have been. Most people took as a matter of course what we have had to learn the hard way, that hap is happy, that mere luck is lucky, and that fortune is fortunate. Their language says it to us – that life is a lottery. We don't know what our lot will be, or what will befall us; but we should be happy to take our chance. So be it.

Martin Heidegger claims that German is the best modern language for philosophy, with its earthy etymologies and homely idioms. We can allow him to contribute here the connection between *Glück* and *Glücklichkeit*, luck and happiness; but that is about all German has to offer. English, that great mongrel, is richer by far. And notice how in each case the supposedly morally neutral notion of random, chance or luck is used in ways that tilt towards a general presumption of *favour*. Yes: the people understand random as *benign*. Only the negative needs a special term: otherwise, to be subject to mere chance is to be *in luck*. Just chance is as often as not a happy chance. We can be happy about hap.

luck	lucky	luckless (c.f., *Glücklos*), unlucky
chance		mischance, perchance
hap	happy	hapless, mishap, perhaps, happening upon
fortune	fortunate	misfortune, unfortunate
fortuitous	fortuity, fortune	
gratuitous	gratuity, grace	

Examples can be multiplied. Notice, for example, the way that fortune means both capricious chance *and* a large sum of money, or perhaps the wealth and security that one may hope for on setting off to London to seek one's fortune.

It is pointed out to me here that although luck, chance, hap, fortune and grace are indeed all of them neutral-but-inclining-to-be-benevolent-and-favourable, there is another group of words that tilt in the opposite direction: hazard, risk, random, peril and jeopardy. I reply that the two groups of words seem to have different uses. We use the luck-and-hap group of words in order to say that it is good to embrace the pure contingency of life and to take what comes, whereas we use the second group of words to warn reckless youth about the folly of gambling and motorcycle racing. The first group of words say that it is blessed to be open and receptive to life, or Being; the second group warns against actively, and perhaps self-destructively, courting danger.

How does it come about that some people describe us as living in a highly regulated and supervised, or providentially-governed, universe, whereas other people are keen to take the opposite view? Perhaps the explanation is that around the world political leaders and the upper classes like to preach to the poor a highly rationalist and literally *laborious* vision of the world. Your local work ethic might be Calvinist or Marxist: either way, you are assured that you are under observation, you are watched, indeed, you are being clocked, life is highly planned and supervised, your merits will not go unnoticed, the system is ultimately benevolent and in the very long term will reward you. Meanwhile, there is no such thing as chance, and in the long run nobody gets away with anything. Very well; but in England the common people have always been healthily sceptical of the moralistic ideologies purveyed to them by their betters, and have always liked to dream of trusting to luck and taking their chances; being *happy-go-lucky*.

One last example of how richly and widely the language pictures the world as disorderly and unplanned: the Latin verb *cadere*, to happen or befall, is perhaps linked with the fall of dice. It gives us not only *incident, accident* and so on, but also *case* (whatever the case turns out to be) and *casual*, and much more besides. Take it easy; every fact is an accident or a happening!

In conclusion, we now see a whole series of themes beginning to fit together. When the focus of religious thought shifts away from God and towards Being, understood as Be(com)ing, we become free to dispense with the idea of a ready-made and objective purpose or Plan in our life. We can give up all the strenuously moralistic and disciplinary work-ethic visions of human life that have been imposed upon the common man since the beginning of history. Original sin, work as a punishment, life spent at hard labour in a vast penitentiary under close supervision – we are happy to be rid of all such ideas. We are free instead to take on board Nietzsche's doctrine of the innocence of Becoming, by which, he says, he redeems the world.[2] Exactly what the last generation feared as 'meaninglessness' begins to look magical. We begin to believe in the graciousness of pure gratuitousness, and the happiness of mere hap.

5. Coming into the world

What is Being's realm or domain, into which it comes and within which it both expresses and conceals itself?

Come to that, do not those *political* metaphors of a realm (*royaume*) or domain (a dominion or lordship) invite the question, Why does there have to be a world in that sense *at all*? Why should we suppose that Being needs to have or looks for a coherent, organized and unified world, a law-governed domain, in which to come to its varied expressions? Why indeed should the One ever 'wish' to become Many, and why should the Many, having become many, then need to backtrack and re-assemble itself into some sort of ordered and coherent totality? Might it not be that the very notion of a *world* – a *universe*, an animal *kingdom*, a *sphere* – is some sort of leftover from the past? Perhaps by suggesting that Being either generates a world, or needs a world to come out into, we may be mistakenly attempting to reinstate ancient monarchical or theological ways of thinking.

Nietzsche evidently thought so. He seems to have abandoned the very notion of Being, and would I think have scorned the modern idea of a Universe on the ground that we have no sufficient reason to think that there is anything that unifies everything. From his point of view our Big Bang, our physical constants and cosmological principles represent theology's last gasp. They indicate that we are still trying to view everything as a single, coherent, law-governed totality. But how do we know there has to be any such thing? Nietzsche has no one-ing of all

47

things, only a turbulent play of conflicting forces. He comes closest to the idea of a world in his early idea of the way each animal, including Man, projects out around itself its own little picture of things by which it lives; and Heidegger appears to be developing that idea in his own conception of *Dasein*, human be-ing, as essentially worldly. We are so constituted that we live and have to live in a world, and with others. In short, we need a field, a mirror, a not-self, a milieu, a *scene:* a stage on which we can come out, act and interact with others. In such a setting we can hope to become (for a little while) ourselves, and perhaps be recognized for what we have become.

In a little more detail, and in passing: Heidegger sees us as living subject to temporality, as radically finite, and therefore as living towards death. We live in a world, with others, speaking (con-versing, to-and-fro-ing). Each of us is an I, a One, concerned about – i.e., responsible for, and with an interest in – our own life, our fate.[1]

Here, we move on somewhat from both Nietzsche and Heidegger. The question raised is, why does Being need to have a world to come out in? Why does there have to be a *world* at all? Indeed, to use an older vocabulary, how might we be able to set about proving the existence of the world? That's a harder and more interesting question than it looks.

In brief, the answer is that there is a world because Being comes forth within language, and language generates a world, the order of the world reflecting the order in language. As grammatical and other rules pervade language and knit it together into a system, so the world is seen as pervaded by a corresponding order; and as language in its movement also reveals an interplay of conflicting forces and points of view, so does the world. (And so does society, and so does the self.) The underlying point is that language itself cannot work unless it is a system, and it already presupposes a world. Linguistic meanings are constructed by drawing lines of distinction across the space of a world. So the position is that we are the world-builders. *We* have to have a world, and the world we have is *our* world, the world we made. We have no reason to think that there is a world absolutely; but *our* world, the multidimensional world we build in language, is good enough to be going on with.[2]

Look where we are now, you and I, on this page. We are in language, in which we are currently making and unmaking worlds. Writing, I position myself in one place in relation to this outflow of words now running out of my pen, and I lose myself in the words as they run. I'm not aware of com-posing, but I watch an outflow. Reading, you position yourself differently, and experience from a different place a (no doubt) somewhat different text. Language must itself move in a multidimensional superworld for such astounding things to be possible within it. So we are in language now, within which on the subjective side there is a play of different viewpoints, angles, interests and even *territories*, and within which also, on the objective side, not just topics and concrete individual things but even entire worlds may come to be and pass away.

So language in motion clears a space within which a network of human interlocutors establish a common public world. Literary media such as the theatre and the novel work as framed miniature re-presentations *in the very same medium* of the way things are in the larger social world. Beautiful idioms in our language also testify to the way the motion of language opens a broad, illuminated and public space: the public realm, articulation, expression, publication, explication, recognition. And then: coming forth, coming to birth, coming out, coming to light, coming out into the open, coming into the world, and broad daylight.

The natal imagery would please Heidegger. While a baby is still in the womb, it is in the dark. We don't know (or used not to know) even what sex it is, or how healthy. But when it has come into the world, all becomes clear (*clarus*, brightly lit). The facts are out in the open, and have become public property. Anyone can tell them, make them out, describe them, bear witness to them.

The first world then, the *real* world, is the broad, illuminated, public space that is opened by our common language. Here we are, in it. There are various rather murky subworlds, such as minds and (metaphorically) wombs, but what is being formed in them remains indeterminate and doubtful until it has come out into the light of common day. The 'light' here mentioned, by the way, is not *lux*, optical light, but the light of conscious awareness which is shed by language. The proceedings in a court of law or at a public inquiry neatly illustrate the way in which within language public truth is publicly brought to light and formally established, in some disputed area. Let language run freely, and let argument and counter-argument run back and forth until a working consensus begins to appear: that is truth, coming to birth.

Suppose you don't agree with me. You read me, but you come to your own somewhat-different conclusions. In that case my claim, that the actual metaphysical situation is entirely congruent with the present situation in these sentences, *still stands!* I have already taken account of your disagreement. Even if you judge me wrong, I'm still right: there is language, and within language there is a broad open space of converse amongst speakers with different angles, interests, powers, capacities, viewpoints. This world of conversation is simply the everyday human life-world within which public truth is established and Being comes to be. Your disagreement with me, as noted just now, is part of the game as I describe it, the game by which truth and reality are produced. *Dis*agreement is only possible *after*, on the basis of, a certain presupposed accord. Concrete existing things in the human life-world are here analysed as made of Be(com)ing, Being coming forth and being formed by the to-and-fro of language. Even by disagreeing with me, you still help me in the building of the common world.

You doubt this? Give me a full and agreed description of any object before you now, with specific measurements locating it in space and time. The description is full, so what extra oomph is needed to bring it to life? Many mathematical physicists have wondered what the difference is, between a complete mathematical description and the real thing, or between an exact replica or perfect automaton and the real thing. Some sort of animating spirit, says ancient thought. Divine power, says Descartes. 'The fire in the equations', says Stephen Hawking. Here, I say that the actual thing is just its own full and definite description in language, filled out or fulfilled by the gentle forthcoming of Be-ing there and then, at that place and in that time, or here and now, as the case may be.

We cannot wholly avoid natal and erotic metaphors here. I make no apology for them: language is like that, and therefore so are we, and we ourselves have no other medium of expression. Being as-it-were 'wants' to come out. The right form of words, well-turned, fresh and elegant, entices or allures Being, draws it forth into expression in and as a being. Be(com)ing rushes into the symbolic form that attracts it, turns it on. Hence our very strong feeling, both in science and poetry, for the formulation that is crisp, neat, and just right.

You have another objection. I know it. You say that this account is crazily anthropocentric. I seem to have built everything around us humans and have qualified everything as being in one way or another made by us and being there for us. Space has become just the space of human interaction, and language has become a set of magic spells by which Being is called forth into the world of beings (because 'man is the shepherd of being'). The world absolutely, it seems, is no more than this humanly-constituted world that has been gradually built up, by us and by the Grace of Being. All this, you say, is wildly anthropocentric.

I reply that this picture of things could only be meaningfully described as being too anthropocentric if any of us could produce a coherent account of some other way that things might be. In fact we know, if we know anything, that we and we alone have evolved all our language, all our knowledge, all our categories of thought, and all our ideas about what is and what is not. We made it all up. Once we understand that everything depends upon language, that we are always inside language, that language is only human and that all our thinking and world-building depend upon language, then radical humanism or thoroughgoing anthropocentrism becomes of course the only option. There is no other. There is not anything for 'Platonism' or metaphysics (for Heidegger, 'metaphysics' = 'Platonism') or realism to be. For me, 'realism' = metaphysics, which equals the belief that something fully independent of our language and of ourselves determines what's real and what's true. But we can have no way of discovering that realism is true. We cannot climb right out of our human condition, and we have no way at all of even beginning to describe a real alternative to it. How could I, in these sentences, climb out of writing, and yet continue to address you? And since there is factually no way that we could know of any other way for things to be, you are not justified in calling me 'unduly' anthropocentric. Instead of 'unduly', one should write, 'unavoidably'. After all, does not the very word *world* mean *wer-ald*, the age of a man? And a Rembrandt who didn't live in 'Rembrandt's world' wouldn't have the means to be Rembrandt. We and our world are so interwoven that we have to be the way our world is, and our world has to be the way we are.

Now I add that by centring this present essay upon the notion of Being I have avoided pure linguistic idealism and pure nihilism. Note that although I have insisted that we *do* make space, we don't make Being, and we don't make time.

True, the word Being is itself an only-human word and part of the language. We have talked about it, and conjured it up. Perhaps in order to flag up the point that Being is a non-word for a non-thing prior to language, it might have been better consistently to have used an obviously anomalous sign like Heidegger's B̶e̶i̶n̶g̶, Derrida's *différance*, or our own Be(com)ing. But as both Heidegger and Derrida are aware, when an anomalous sign is used consistently, it is brought under a *nomos* or law and so ceases to be anomalous. It becomes normalized, and so becomes just somebody's technical term, a bit of jargon and even a trendy buzzword. To avoid that difficulty, we need to keep changing our terminology a little: ~~Being~~, Be-ing, Being's coming forth, Be(com)ing, E-vent, the Fountain. As we strive to establish a common world and a common truth, it is that gentle contingent forthcomingness that flows out to fill our language. By our language it is differentiated into a shared public world. It is our partner, our collaborator.

Notice that whereas God is a transcendent super-Male who insists on controlling everything and laying down the Law, some people will undoubtedly see Being as super-feminine, easy, close by us, discreet, amenable, and quietly taking on the shape of that to which she is drawn, lured, enticed, shepherded. She is a womb, the womb of time; she is an in-turning or *Einkehr* (Heidegger); a *chora* or vessel (Kristeva and Irigaray); she is a matrix of possibilities (from *mater*, Derrida). She creates, not by imposing her will, but by self-giving. I shall not develop this suggestion further, beyond repeating what has been said already: our language is radically human, as human as our very bodies are. Every piece of writing, and certainly every piece of writing that is concerned with the arts and humanities, with ethics and politics, always conveys messages about the body, the emotions, human relationships and gender. And why not? But the result is that insofar as we think *about* Being, we will anthropomorphize it, or her – which, by the way, is why I have suggested that we should see Being as (poetically) human: *human Being*, in a new sense. Human Being.

The point just raised, however, has some relevance to a final question. Whereas Heidegger gives Being a history and is ready (one hopes, metaphorically) to ascribe to her quite complex strategies of self-revelation and self-concealment, I have rather portrayed Being as constant. (You just can't avoid sexism, can you?) Like a fountain, Being is an even, temporally-continuous forthcoming of pure contingency – ever in motion, always the same. But in that case, how does plurality and a conflict of forces enter the world? If the world is deeply at odds with itself, how does it manage to remain in Being?

Almost every possible theory has been advanced. One

philosopher, Schopenhauer, has attributed a measure of objective plurality and conflict to the Will, the noumenal reality of the world, which is for him nothing but blind, aimless driving energy, ignorant of whether it is or is not at odds with itself. Here we do not agree with Schopenhauer. Being is simple and constant. That said, we turn to the world of phenomena, and within it distinguish four levels: the self, language, society and nature. At each of these four levels, we hope to see *a world*, that is, a certain unity and overall law-abidingness that (just about) succeeds in containing disruptive and conflicting forces. But we also tend to see one of the four levels as being basic. That basic region is the site where the virus of painful and perhaps self-destructive internal conflict first takes hold, and then sub-sequently spreads to the other three levels. Where is this basic site? It is the eternal conflict of points of force in Nature, says Nietzsche; it is the conflict of forces within and between States, say Machiavelli, Hobbes and others; it is the conflict of biological drives within the human psyche, says Freud; it is the conflict of forces that can be traced in every text, says Derrida.

I have adumbrated a different view, closer to modern biology, by saying that whereas Being gives us temporality, we ourselves make space. As we converse, we make it as *territory*. Watch the way birdsong establishes territories in springtime: the law is that *every utterance not only communicates information to the hearer, but also stakes out a claim by the speaker*, a claim to living-space, a territory. And there is more: because the bird's utterance is – and has to be – couched in a vocabulary intelligible to other members of his species, it also works as an offer of peace. Each bird in effect says: 'Here I am, and this is my territory, which I will defend. But I don't need any more than this. Why not move in next door? Then, if you respect my territory I'll respect yours, for that also is the Law.' And so all the land is settled peacefully and efficiently, by a combination of assertion, threat and promise.

In some such way, surely, human conversation tends to mark

out and occupy moral and political space, and to generate a common, public world. A real world, the world of Be(com)ing.

6. Being and nihilism

In the very earliest vision of life that we can trace, human beings were not very clearly aware of living in a *world* at all. They experienced existence simply as a dense scrimmage of conflicting Powers, some hostile, some indifferent and some friendly. The frontier between the human self and the surrounding environment was ill-defined, and the scrimmage rolled back and forth across it regardless. The disorderly flux of life was therefore seen as being subject to sudden changes of fortune and magical transformations.

In such a milieu, people saw life pretty much as a street child in a Third-World city sees it today: you battled for survival and you lived by your wits. That is why the earliest and most universal type of culture-hero around the world is the Trickster.[1] He above all is the character we love and admire. He is the ultimate survivor: he always escapes. He is almost immortal. He can trick his way out of any situation, solve any riddle, survive any ordeal. He makes us smile; he can get away with cheating even the very gods themselves. He isn't a strong man at all; indeed, he is often physically slight. But his wits always come to his rescue, and we identify with him. Not only is he very archaic, but a lot of him remains in Abraham and Odysseus, in Robin Hood and Charlie Chaplin, and in the adventure-heroes of our present-day popular entertainment.

Of much more recent origin than the Trickster is a very different sort of culture-hero, the Wise Man. He first appears as a lawgiver, at the time when the first state societies arose. He is old and bearded; he is Manu, Solon, Hammurabi, Confucius, Moses. He may be pictured as being a king, or a king's counsellor, or a judge or a priest. He represents the point of view of the new ruling class within the state. He portrays human life as lived *in an ordered world*, which means that we live, not in wild Nature, but subject to law, in a law-governed domain or realm. His notion of law is very wide-ranging, as it still remains even to this day, for it includes not only religious law, the civil law and the moral law, but even standards of rationality and physical regularities – the laws of logic and the laws of nature. Astonishingly, every major field of study and sphere of life is still today perceived as being a law-governed little realm, just like the state. It is still true, not only that 'man is a political animal', but that all of human thought is modelled on politics.

The Wise Man teaches a ruling-class vision of the world and of human life, and he practises what he preaches, because he is an example of self-mastery. He has learnt self-knowledge and self-discipline, and he shows us by his own conduct that not only the city-state and the cosmos but also the human self works best and most harmoniously when it is brought under the rule of law. Again the Wise Man shows his predilection for wide-ranging, world-spanning analogies: reason should be the sovereign legislator within the self, just as the king is in the state, and God in the cosmos.

The Wise Man has then been a favourite culture-hero of the ruling class since early-Bronze-Age times, whereas the Trickster, the Buster Keaton figure, has been and still remains the culture-hero of the common people. The Wise Man's universe is a harmonious cosmos governed by law at every level, a carefully designed world with built-in and objective universal standards of goodness and rationality. That's what we are enjoined to believe in; that's what we must create – and we create it by behaving as if it actually exists. By contrast, the Trickster's universe is scarcely a *uni*-verse at all: he experiences only a disorderly play of forces and course of events, amidst which he survives by his own joyous resourcefulness and wit. The Trickster's great advantage is that his experience of life is very much more direct and intense. His joys and sorrows are very *fierce*. In Heideggerian terms, it might be said that he lives in Being. He is instantly responsive; he skips and dances with the *turn* of events. (Forget linear time: think of the stream of events as twisting and turning like a writhing snake.) Often, he is a footballer, or an acrobat, a tumbler. As for the Wise Man, he sees the world through the spectacles of a great deal of metaphysical theory. He sees a *cosmos*, *substances*, *laws* in operation, *standards* being observed, etc. The Wise Man experiences Being only as the Being of beings – i.e., as hidden within beings. He is not *solar*; he does not *feel* life, so much as theorize it and legislate for it. He doesn't *burn*; he is too cool.

There is next to be noted a further important difference between these two world-views. One of them is *de*scriptive, and the other is *pre*scriptive. The Trickster's vision represents life as the overwhelming majority of human beings have always actually experienced it. He tells the truth about life: that life is chaotic, Rabelaisian, wildly capricious and with many sudden and unmerited ups-and-downs of fortune. But we do not complain. We make the best of things; we use our wits: somehow the Trickster always survives, and so will we. By contrast, the Wise Man's vision represents the point of view of civilization, and in particular of the tiny ruling-class élite. The Wise Man is an apologist. He seeks to justify belief in a *world*, a harmonious law-governed cosmos. He seeks to justify political obligation, self-mastery and universal moral and intellectual standards. He tries to persuade us that we will all of us be much better off if we can together contrive to get belief in these things socially established and as widely recognized and enforced as possible. He wants conformity. He tells us to see the world, not as it is, but as it is our (literally) *civic* duty to see it.

Now, to which of these two parties do the philosophers belong? The answer is obvious: in all ages, and especially from Plato to Kant, nearly all the philosophers have been Wise Men, apologists for law and order, defenders of civilization, rationalists and moral realists. There have always been a few cynics and sceptics, poets and playwrights, to voice the low-life Trickster's point of view, but naturally the vast majority of religious and academic intellectuals have always been proponents of the Wise Man's teachings. Only in the nineteenth century, as culture becomes more democratized and thinking becomes more historically-aware, does the low person's view of life begin to be taken seriously. After Hegel it begins to be suggested that reality might actually be produced, not by a solitary, wise legislating Monarch, but as the outcome of an interplay of non-rational forces. This in due course gives rise to a typically nineteenth-century paradox: philosophers like Schopenhauer and Nietzsche go on being right-wing élitists, keen on high culture, authority and strong government, just like so many other philosophers before them. But now they find themselves obliged to combine their élitism with an increasingly tricksterish view of the actual human condition; and from their cultural-social élitist standpoint, tricksterism looks to be an embarrassingly crude and low-class view of life. The trickster's picture of the human condition seems to mock the 'lofty' aesthetic and cultural values that they treasure. The result in Schopenhauer is an almost suicidal pessimism that aims flatly to deny nature, or 'the Will', by turning it back against itself. In Nietzsche, the result is nihilism, and a terrific struggle on his part to say Yes to life in the face of it. It is not easy to be an aristocratic trickster.

The nineteenth-century intellectual (I am suggesting) was very often driven to pessimism or nihilism by the death of 'the Cosmos'; that is, by her growing conviction that the nature of things does nothing at all to support and much to under-mine the optimistic vision of the world – as being rational and morally-supervised – that religion and civilization have always instructed her to believe in. Excellent examples of all this are to be found in Emily Brontë, George Eliot, Matthew Arnold, Thomas Hardy, and others. A French counterpart might be Zola, an example of the sort of person who cares deeply for moral and high-cultural values, but who knows that *in fact* we are merely the products of an interplay of blind forces, forces that continue to toss us about unthinkingly.

The same difficulty – the death of 'the Cosmos' – has continued to trouble twentieth-century intellectuals. If the values of civilization can no longer claim any cosmic endorsement, how do you justify morality and how do you justify political obligation? For most of the twentieth century the problem has looked so severe that a great many intellectuals – including Heidegger – have fallen into very harsh forms of political authoritarianism.

However, I am going to disagree sharply with the pessimism and the passive nihilism of these middle-class literary intellectuals. They misread their situation absurdly. They failed to see that the great block of realistically-understood metaphysical and religious beliefs that had prevailed from Plato to Kant had always functioned simply as 'civil' or 'political' ideology. From Plato's *Republic* and *Timaeus* to Paley's *Natural Theology*, very much the same complex of beliefs – in a good and wise Creator, in a rationally-coherent cosmos with a built-in moral order, in the immortality of the soul and in the ultimate triumph of Justice – had been propagated by the upper-class defenders of civilization in order to persuade the common people to be loyal to civilization. It was necessary to convince the people of the well-planned benevolence of the whole system within which they were living. Inevitably, the preachers had always issued dire warnings about the frightful consequences of failure to hold fast to these beliefs. It was considered a 'political' duty to believe in universal objective standards of rationality and goodness, to believe in the ultimate unity of the most-real and the most-good, and so on. Indeed, it is still just such a duty. To this day, if you find yourself wanting to question or reject standard Enlightenment conceptions of Reason, the unity of morality, experience, the objectivity of knowledge and so forth, you will find yourself in trouble for *heresy*. You are just *wrong*; you are politically disloyal, subversive and immoral. That is to say, our regnant philosophical orthodoxy has exactly the same status and is defended in exactly the same basically-political ways as our regnant religious orthodoxy. Our philosophy is not philosophy but politics, and our religion is not religion but politics; and despite all appearances to the contrary, the two remain curiously complicit, especially at Oxbridge. So, as all this began to come apart during the nineteenth century, many middle-class intellectuals became extremely gloomy. They had truly believed their own ideology because they were themselves its chief beneficiaries, and now they couldn't see how life could go on without it. But they absurdly over-estimated the merits of the beliefs that were now collapsing, and they failed to remember something that the very greatest writers have always known – that the common people had never really bought the ideology of civilization. They were not taken in. They had never benefited all that much from it. Indeed, it was never intended to benefit *them* very much. So they have always known that the Trickster's vision of life is factually correct, and they have always delighted in the Trickster's high spirits. They get far more religious happiness out of watching the agility of Buster Keaton getting away with it, than from hearing the preacher assure them that they will *not* get away with it. Of course the Trickster gets away with it; and notice that he is everywhere portrayed as being an immortal. In ballads and novels, in comic shorts and cartoons, there is never a Trickster's death-scene, except as yet another trick. The stories about him can be multiplied for ever.

I now have a second observation to make about middle-class pessimism, which may be summed up in the following question: 'If nihilism is a Bad Thing, why is it that the Dalai Lama is such a happy man and the Pope is such an unhappy man?' For basically political reasons, I have been saying, our Western tradition has always insisted that a complex set of dogmatic beliefs in metaphysics and in religion are collectively essential to culture, to our present happiness and our final salvation. But we have also had a minority tradition going back through people like David Hume to Sextus Empiricus in antiquity, which says that philosophical and religious dogmatism is damaging.[2] Although it extols universal Reason, dogmatism cannot actually *itself* be fully justified by the same Reason that it commends (just as the Pope cannot defend his own infallibility by appealing to it), and dogmatism therefore tends to make us into difficult and unhappy people. The best way to happiness is to suspend judgment upon all such speculative questions. We do best if we simply accept appearances undogmatically, and live 'naturally', going with the flow and peaceably following the local way of life. In a word, the less you believe, the calmer you are and the better able to respond to others. The less you believe, the more you will be in touch with your own feelings and able to live by the heart, responsive to the promptings of life and able to accept and affirm things as they are.

In brief then, the reason why the Pope is poetically unhappy is that he is caught in a philosophical contradiction. He must be an objective rationalist, someone for whom there is but one absolute Reason and universal *raison d'être*, out-there in the divine Mind; but he knows that this belief cannot itself be rationally justified to the general satisfaction without presupposing itself, and it must nowadays be maintained simply by an exertion of the authority of his office. This, however, has the effect of separating the official from the private man. The unfortunate Karol Wojtyla is the only human being on earth who has no Pope to look to, to sustain his faith. No wonder he is unhappy. Who will be the Pope's Pope?

By contrast, the Dalai Lama's religion is sceptical and therapeutic. In metaphysics, he follows the Buddha and Nagarjuna. He truly believes, in Nothing. He is happy in the emptiness of Emptiness. He is not institutionally obliged either to hold or to purvey to others any false beliefs at all. Even of his own great office, he remarks now only that it will continue if the Tibetan people want it to continue; and if not, not. O lucky man, sceptical saint, holy nihilist, true un/believer! Why isn't a Christian allowed to be like that?

Against this background we can now begin to understand how and why Heidegger asserts that our modern Western nihilism can be seen as the first stage of a new revelation of Being. Since Plato and Aristotle, the West has been dominated by various forms of metaphysical realism, and more recently by technological or instrumental thinking. We have held a highly-ideological belief in a law-governed and controllable – i.e., manipulable – surrounding world of beings-out-there. We have increasingly seen everything in terms of power and control. All our thinking has been about the Law, cosmic and social. We have been utterly obsessed with political and technical power, to such an extent that the primal, abyssal question of Being itself has been entirely hidden and forgotten.

True, for Heidegger, 'Being is the Being of beings': that is, Being is present in an expressed, objectified and therefore heavily-occluded way in the Wise Man's orderly world of law-abiding beings. But now, with the Death of God and the end of metaphysics, twentieth-century people are deprived even of a veiled and degraded experience of Being; and it might therefore seem that our loss of Being has now become absolute. Heidegger, though, replies that now that we have lost even the lower-level and mediated access to Being that we used to have through theistic realism and metaphysics, the only possibility left to us is a fresh experience of Being itself in all its primitive and overwhelming purity.

So it's next stop the pre-Socratics, and hello Heraclitus? One begins to see why it is that in German expressionist art from Otto Dix to Beuys, Baselitz and Kiefer, and recently in some even more extreme London artists such as Marc Quinn and Damien Hirst, there is a conscious attempt to return into the archaic and to explore the most violent feelings of horror, dread and disgust. As ascetics once tortured themselves in the hope of forcing God to act, and as terrorists still try to force the coming of the revolution, so these artists are trying to push nihilism so far as to force the new and awaited revelation of Being. If you think that making art out of body fluids, excreta and fragments of human corpses is a trifle extreme, you should remember that we live in an era when perhaps the majority of people never,

ever, aspire beyond a sitcom view of life. After the Death of
Man, galvanism is an excusable way of attempting resuscita-
tion.

We can now consider three possible interpretations of
Heidegger's project, and of what he may mean by Being.

The first line of interpretation suggests that in seeking to
return into a pre-metaphysical and pre-Socratic form of consciousness, Heidegger is seeking to take us back from the Wise
Man's to something more like the Trickster's view of the human
condition. One commentator, Hilary Lawson, is so bold as
to detect an extensive use of the Trickster's stratagems in
Heidegger's own murky text:[3] but however that may be,
certainly there is a great deal of tricksterism in Nietzsche's *Fröh-
liche Wissenschaft*, and Heidegger was profoundly indebted to
Nietzsche. Here, too, one thinks of the pervasiveness of the
dance as metaphor in twentieth-century art and thought from
Picasso, Matisse, Stravinsky and Diaghilev onwards. That
people are well able to recognize the Trickster as a religious
figure is shown, not only by the Gospel stories that depict Jesus
himself as a trickster outwitting the enemies who seek to entrap
him, but also by the modern popularity of Christ and Siva as
Lords of the Dance, and of Krishna as a Trickster-divinity. The
Trickster is almost a symbol of spirit: he continually achieves
liberation, frees himself by skipping clear of the forces that surround him and seek to crush him. He eludes capture, he dances
free like Bugs Bunny (who, as you will recall, is himself actually
called a trickster in the cartoon 'Hare Tonic' of 1945), and he
thereby shows the stupidity of reason. Reason is clunking one-
level calculation, of a kind that a computer can easily copy. As
I write, a computer has just beaten Kasparov at chess. But no
mere computer could ever emulate the Trickster. The Trickster
is magical. He is a wit, he has native wit, he has his wits about
him. So it is just possible that when Nietzsche and Heidegger
criticize one-eyed Socratic metaphysical Reason and seek to lead
us back to something older and greater, we should see them as
trying to lead us back from the Wise Man's world-view to the

Trickster's. Our twentieth-century culture is dominated by the State and the Law, by routinization and by technological rationality. Already, we could be governed entirely by computers – and perhaps we are. For that matter, we could ourselves be replaced by computers – and perhaps we will be. Neo-Tricksterism could be *exactly* the religious message we now need, showing a nihilistic age the only remaining way to spiritual liberation.

A second line of interpretation of Heidegger's project begins by asking what exactly he means by Being. Often he equates Being with the abyssal *question* of Being, the *Seinsfrage*. In which case, he is using the word Being, not to designate or point to anything at all, but rather to evoke an emotion of cosmic awe and dread at the Emptiness of all existence. Reason fails. We cannot calculate the void. And this overwhelming experience of the nothingness that underlies everything calls our entire life into question, and relativizes all human achievements and institutions. In the void, we are stripped of all certainties and forced to become creative. We find the strength to create new gods, found new cities, and make new works of art.

I am suggesting here that we may read Heidegger's talk of Being in a Hobbesian and 'non-cognitive' way. Talk of Being is intended to evoke a feeling of deep metaphysical horror that utterly destroys an old world-view and obliges us to set about creating a new one.

We turn now to the third possible line of interpretation of Heidegger's message about Being. It sees Heidegger as a transcendental philosopher, just as Rudolphe Gasché and others have also tried to interpret Derrida as a transcendental philosopher. Being is transcendental. It is 'in back': it is always presupposed. It is prior to the distinction between Being and Becoming. It is prior to the distinctions between being and non-being, and between something and nothing. Being is that ungraspable transcendental thing prior to language which language always presupposes but can never properly capture – and if so, then 'Being' itself cannot quite be a proper word, and should rather be put 'under erasure' and written ~~Being~~. Being is the unknowable no-thing prior to language and prior to existence that opens up the whole field of existence. So there is no sense in asking 'Is Being some-thing or is it no-thing?', because to phrase the question in that way shows that you've missed the point. Being really is prior to the something/nothing distinction. It is radically anomalous and elusive, *itself* a bit tricksterish.

Try again: the whole world of beings comes forward into being all the time, and is 'given' to us. It is such a pure gift that there is no giver: that's *really* gratuitous. It comes from nowhere. We've abandoned metaphysics, and all the old ideas of substance. So *what* is it all, *how* is it all, and anyway, *where* is it all coming from – or is there really no 'where' whence it comes? So to talk about Being is to talk about an abyssal, mysterious, everywhere-and-always givenness that is 'systematically' elusive. Talk about Being is prompted by the question, 'How is all this so?' Answer: it just is, it gives, it happens, it *comes to pass*. More than that, it is so transient that it never stops: coming, it is already passing.

While a film is showing you can't see the screen: you see only the dance of appearances *on* the screen, which gives rise to the attractive illusion of people-in-a-world. But when the film ends the picture house is in pitch darkness, and you *still* can't see the screen. So the screen is never seen at all – either while the film is showing, or during the sudden total darkness and silence that follows its ending.

Think about that parable. Within the parable, it is presumed that we already know that there are such things as screens. We've seen them, in fact. Whereas, if our actual life-situation is like that, we can never know it and will never know it. That may be how things are, but we'll never know.

Now, if you are a person who is serious about philosophy and religious thought, thinking about this parable should have caused you to shiver a little and I hope feel extremely sick with metaphysical horror. On my second, 'Hobbesian' or emotivist, interpretation of Heidegger that shiver of horror is Being. The question of the screen is somehow real but *metaphysically* un-answerable, and so fills one with abyssal dread or horror. This isn't agnosticism, but the truly sickening thought that we may be metaphysically and irredeemably locked into alienation from truth.

Alternatively you may have imagined a couple of Woody-Allen-type characters within the film being shown on the screen, arguing that there must be *something* that sustains the crazy dance of flickering appearances in which they find themselves caught up. But it must be radically different from the appearances that it sustains, otherwise it wouldn't do any sustaining. So there must be some underlying support, but we can know nothing about it.

In so arguing, our imaginary characters are approximating to my third, and transcendental, interpretation of what Heidegger's talk about Being may amount to.

On the Tricksterish interpretation, Heidegger was acutely aware of modern culture's drive towards world domination, global technology and total war. He traces the origins of theoretical and technical rationality and of our preoccupation with power back to Plato. His talk about Being is intended to reawaken a very ancient, pre-theoretical kind of thinking, the Trickster's lightness of foot, that will help us to escape from the destruction into which we are heading. And indeed, Tricksterish thinking was once prominent in the great religious traditions – such as, for example, Judaism and Zen Buddhism.

On the Horrid interpretation, Heidegger's talk of B̶e̶i̶n̶g̶ is to be understood purely emotively and non-cognitively. Being is simply the question of Being, whose function is to give us the horrors, and thereby to unmake us and oblige us to remake ourselves and our world.

On the Transcendental interpretation, Being under erasure, Being, is a radically unknowable ineffable non-thing, a primal Ground (*Urgrund*) that is always presupposed, always behind our backs but never seen. We see the all-the-time-givenness of things – but the *giving?* No. And this radical, systematic elusiveness of Being should warn us *not* to make the gross mistake of projecting quasi-human attributes upon it and turning it into some kind of relaunch of the old God.

Other interpretations of what's meant by talk of Being could be offered here, and I mention one in particular. It is my own, already presented: the 'Japanese' interpretation. On this view Be-ing, or Be(com)ing, is just about the same thing as temporality. Being is everything's continual self-replacement just in time, everything's state of ongoing coming-into-being-and-passing-away. Time carries things away so quickly that everything keeps running in order to stand still, and that running is its Be-ing.

Here we differ interestingly from those many painters and photographers who have in various ways sought to capture – or 'freeze' – the passing moment. Is that not a form of *fetishism*, which is in relation to the relation of Being what idolatry is in relation to the religion of God? We should not try to *capture* the fleeting moment; we should *kiss* it as it flies. Being is transient, and to let Being be we must let it go. This letting-go that lets things be Heidegger calls 'releasement towards things', *gelassenheit*. And why does pure transience make one happy? Think of a child's pleasure in battling against a gusty wind that is blowing everything away, and think of the phrase 'gales of levity'. Reverse Milan Kundera's erroneous book-title, and think of the *Blissful* Lightness of Being. Being's gift of itself is the purest gift of all, because there is no giver; and our response of thanksgiving is the purest and most religious thanksgiving of all, because there is nobody there to thank.

That makes *four* interpretations, then. Academic commentators sometimes talk as if Heidegger 'ought' to hold, and to stick to, just one of them. They want language to be dead, with fixed meanings, and they want philosophers to be pedants. But Being is not like that; and in any case language in general is not like that. According to Heidegger himself Being is systematically elusive, so it is not surprising that there are a number of strands in his own use of the term. Being is such that there cannot be a certain way of speaking about it that pins it down and gets it right. But in addition, with the end of the Platonic era we have come generally to recognize that there is no such thing as *the* meaning of a word. Words are products of history, and each of them has over the years gathered a whole range of effective possible uses.

In summary, then, we should not ask either Heidegger, or even this present text, to be rigidly self-consistent. There is no one ready-made Truth of things out there, no Right Answer to each and every question waiting for us, and no one true meaning of each word. We make it all up. A philosophical text is a sort of artwork, and a touch of pluralism and metaphorical richness is a good thing. We should not make the mistake of writing as if we think that our word is or could be the very last word.

To take matters further, we turn next to the relation of Being to language.

7. Being and language

In Hans Christian Andersen's story, the Emperor walking out in procession had a visible body but no visible clothes. In H.G. Wells's story, the Invisible Man had to be completely swathed in clothes to make him visible at all. Put the two stories side-by-side, and we have a neat parable of contrasting views about the relation between language and reality, clothing and the body, Culture and Nature. In Andersen's story, what is seen is bare Nature: in the Wells story, bare Nature as such is invisible, and in order to become visible must be swathed in linguistic or cultural wrappings.

Ordinary people – along with most ordinary scientists – are Andersenites, or realists. They simply don't see the world as being swathed in language: on the contrary, they think that the unbiassed human observer directly perceives a fully-formed naked real world out there, just as it is. Certainly the Emperor needs to be clothed and made culturally decent, but that is because we can already see only too clearly *exactly* what shape he is without any clothes on.

Other people – many writers, artists and philosophers – are nowadays Wellsians. Their point of view is 'culturalist' and anti-realist. They believe that naked reality, if *per impossible* it could ever be encountered, would be completely formless, invisible and unintelligible. Not only the Invisible Man, but everything in the world about us has had to be wrapped about with language, swaddled and swathed with descriptions and interpretations, so that it can be incorporated into the human world: so that it can be *brought into the conversation* of humanity. Contrary to what the plain person supposes, it is in the first place *words* that call things into being: or rather, that call Being forth into things. It is words that shape things, describe them, define them, delineate them, outline them. It is only because words have first differentiated and illuminated the world that, *secondarily*, graphic artists can come along and trace the outlines of things. Verbal delineation precedes graphic delineation. And a world differentiated and formed by human language is a humanly-appropriated world, a functioning *social* world, a world of human communication. We may compare this, say the Wellsians, with the way the Invisible Man has had to wrap himself up completely in his clothes, his dark glasses, bandages and false nose, so that he can then talk normally to other people.

Notice that each of these parties sees only one thing. The commonsensical Andersenites see only Nature, believing themselves to be in direct contact with objective reality. They are not very aware of language, seeing it as merely copying or tracing the structure of a ready-made world that is already fully-formed before we have said a word. By contrast, the Wellsians see only language. For them the world is empty, a pathless waste, until language has come along and formed it, differentiated it, shaped it, and made it humanly intelligible. The known human world exists only within language. Because we think in language, we see the world by reading it. We see and hear *through words*. Listen to the news for a week, read the daily press for a week, and there you will have in your own hands a neat illustration of the way the world is built within language. When you have seen how your knowledge of everything that lies beyond your own immediate horizon is constructed entirely within language, you may be half-way to recognizing that the same is also true of your everyday surroundings. Teach your child to speak, and watch its world take shape.

If you are not convinced yet, consider the way taxonomists establish in language a standard description of each newly-

discovered species of animal and plant. Once the new species –
of butterfly, perhaps – has been definitely described, it has
become part of the language and can be referred to again. Now
multiply this up by considering all our varied registries, certifi-
cates, charts, patents, standards, maps and dictionaries, and you
begin to see to what an extent we do and must establish standard identifying descriptions and definitions of everything. The
whole world is on file: the whole world is like the Internet – a
huge communications network which draws upon a number of
great databases. Be(com)ing is the coming-forth of the objective
common world within the humming web of our communication. Always, the proximate thing, the very first thing you see,
is an activated meaning, which you may see bulging up as if
pregnant when a being emerges within it.

Brilliantly simple and clear illustrations of this point are to be
found in the works of Victor Vasarely (1908-96). In several
works of the 1930s Vasarely practises an early form of Op Art.
He paints a pattern of stripes, slightly distorted in such a way
that the eye can read it as outlining a pair of tigers or zebras
fighting. He paints a checked pattern, again in such a way that
the eye reads it as a soft cloth laid over a solid body: the distor-
tion of the checkerboard pattern reveals the shape of a manikin
bulging up beneath it.[1] Philosophically, these works can be read
as Wittgensteinian: they show us how the eye actively inter-
prets the visual stimuli presented to it. We try out an object-
hypothesis, we see the picture *as* this or that. But more than
that, Vasarely's works are parables of the way an individual
being bulges up and emerges from a continuous background
matrix of meaning. That is it! – that is how the 'real world'
before us comes out in language, or is produced by and against
a background of language. The flowing one-level world of
linguistic meaning is like a 'coat of many colours', a soft textile
laid over the world which, like drapery in classical sculpture,
reveals the shape and the movements of the body beneath.
'When as in silks my Julia goes', sings Robert Herrick, 'Then,
then, methinks, how sweetly flows / The liquefaction of her

clothes', but don't get distracted; concentrate on the insight that 'reality' – the world of beings – emerges within language, or shows through the movement, the *slippage* of language.

Is Woman a natural Wellsian, who sees the world in terms of clothing, surfaces, appearances, flowing meanings and speculative interpretations, whereas Man is a natural Andersenite, who rudely casts aside all appearances and seeks to penetrate the naked Truth of things? I mean, is the contrast between the two philosophies one that is *already* deeply built into our culture? Are the two philosophies locked in mutual squabbles and misunderstandings, but also mutual need and complementarity, like the two sexes? Some nineteenth-century writers seem to have thought so. But their projection of radically different worldviews upon the two sexes now seems dated and unsatisfactory. Instead, let us say simply that the Andersenites see one thing and the Wellsians another. The Andersenites see objective reality out there and are scarcely aware of language at all; the Wellsians see meanings. They see words. They see the world as coming-to-be within language and language as being outsideless. There really *is* a world-wide-web of language: *linguistic* cyberspace has always existed. The Andersenites see only the body, the Wellsians see only the clothing. The Andersenites see a world of naked facts; the Wellsians see a world of covers and discoveries, veils and revelations, clothes, masks and conflicting interpretations.

Two radically different world-views, one straight and the other indirect, one realistic and the other non-realist. But which of them is *the truth*? Unfortunately the two world-views are so profoundly different that they have very different ideas about what truth is. The 'male' realist goes 'straight' to 'the point'. He believes in naked Truth. But the 'gay', female or 'deviant' nonrealist says that naked truth is never quite reached. Behind each veil there is always another veil; we are always within language. With Nietzsche, the non-realist says that 'there are no facts, only interpretations';[2] with Rorty he says that 'interpretation goes all the way down'. There is of course a publicly-constructed and brightly-lit common world; but we made it, and it is held within and seen through our language. We recognize beings, bulging through the surface of language, Be-ing away: but again, we are *not* to claim objective or absolute knowledge. Capital-B Being, we may say, 'presents' itself to us, in our words, our world. Try reading 'presents' with the accent, first on the first syllable, and then on the second: and then – leave it at that! The Wellsian will never claim actually to see the naked imperial Truth. He says we've got to give up that idea; whereas the Andersenite says that above all else that that notion of bare fact is exactly what we must hold on to. He cannot and he will not live without his highly-political dream of objective reality and objective truth, out-there and independent of us, sovereign over us.

How does one negotiate such a deep disagreement? The Wellsians have a tough time. Their point of view is little more than a century old, and still has problems establishing its own legitimacy.[3] Since Nietzsche (or alternatively perhaps, since the young Hegelians) they have been trying to establish a new philosophical vocabulary and a new view of the world, after Plato and after the Death of God. But it is still not clear whether we will ever succeed in finally laying Plato's ghost. Long habit, traditional belief, established idioms, and to a considerable extent language itself keep on whispering the names of Plato and Aristotle in our ears, and dragging us back into realism (= 'metaphysics', = 'Platonism'). With established idioms within the language so often tilted against us, how are we Wellsians to explain our point of view without seeming to everyone to fall into self-inconsistency, vile obscurity, or evasiveness, or difficulty, or wild excess, or just plain craziness? (Every major Wellsian seems to be accused of at least *two* of these sins; check the names of Nietzsche, Wittgenstein, Heidegger and Derrida, to start with.)

The point of view I am proposing is this: I am both ridiculously 'male' – or so I am assured – and incurably 'Wellsian', so I feel a need to resolve a conflict. Like other Wellsians, I hold that the plain commonsense view of the world is badly wrong and urgently needs to be updated. In particular, traditional realistic styles of thinking in morality and religion are now painfully mistaken and ill-fitting. But these are just the areas of life where philosophy is for everybody, and therefore most needs to be democratic (i.e., intelligibly-written). My best recourse, then, is just to go on explaining the Wellsian point of view in the simplest and most explicit language I can find, until one by one people begin to admit that it does after all make much better and more coherent sense of life as we nowadays live it. In particular, it is consistent with the fact that it is *itself* put forward in language. So I must simply talk on and on until you drop off your perch.

The democratic method – clear writing – is not altogether new. Nietzsche, William James and Richard Rorty have all used it to excellent effect. Heidegger, of course, is a byword for atrocious obscurity, and if he is often being referred to here it is because of the almost Tricksterish cleverness of his central strategy: he calls realism 'metaphysics' or 'Platonism', and presents his own non-realism in the form of a philosophy of Being; and he does all this so craftily that even Catholic theologians take him to be almost one of themselves and pile in to take advantage of him. He will have the last laugh, as the next step in the argument will show.

From our Wellsian point of view, reality is an ever-changing human construct ('man is the shepherd of Being'). We build it within language ('language is the house of Being'). It is our brightly-lit common, public world, before you now, and in your field of view. But reality (the 'real world') is like one of those old Volkswagen Beetle cars, in being *rear-engined*. The motive energy that drives it, Being's Be(com)ing, is always behind us, 'in back', out of sight, always presupposed, but never actually in view. We may compare the language-generating area of the brain within the transmission of the car. As it comes forth, e-ventuates, Be(com)ing gets formed, determined, shaped by language. Then it pours out into expression as our world. (The point being, of course, that we make our world exactly as God does in Genesis.)

But can we get out, go round the back of the car, lift the rear hood, and take a look at the engine? What is Being in itself, prior to any determination by language? Tautologically, it is no thing describable. There is no thing there whose existence might attract remark and call for explanation, and there is no founding Ground. Prior to language, Be(com)ing is empty, slipping pure contingency – the words functioning as a sort of sieve that drips a little, but retains nothing. We are talking, not pseudo-negative theology, but genuine negative theology.

An important point needs to be made here. Aristotle, asking what matter is prior to any determination by form, says that it is of course indeterminate (*aoriston*). Well, that's a tautology. But sure enough, the Indeterminate finds itself getting determined as a sort of gas or soup, just as in our own day some people insist upon identifying unidentified flying objects as UFOs, and then building a mythology around them. Human beings have an unquenchable lust for idols. But it really is philosophically important that when we speak of Being we confine ourselves to what I'm calling 'sieve-phrases', forms of words that hold nothing; forms of words that do no more than point in the direction of something that all language presupposes but that always eludes language. It is the O-Void, the vent from which everything E-Ventuates. But only the outcome is ever seen; that from which the outcome comes out is never seen.[4]

Now we ask about Time the same question that we have just asked about Being. Humans impose upon temporality an extremely rich and complex differentiation. We think of time as passing away, of time as linear, of time as travelling in a certain direction, of time as moving forward like an earthworm, ingesting the future while it is simultaneously depositing behind itself the past. We impose upon time a great range of periodicities, derived from our own biology, from the rhythms of the seasons, from history, and from religion.

But what is Time *prior* to all human cultural-linguistic structuring? What is Time out in the deepest space? Again, the answer has to be that it is nothing but pure empty slipping temporality, going nowhere – another sieve-phrase, which shows that we cannot tell the difference between Being-in-itself and Temporality-in-itself. They converge. We have come to the same no-thing. For the time being, Being and Time are indistinguishable – in being Nothing.

We now get a clearer view of the relationship between non-realism and nihilism. The non-realist (or Wellsian) says that we do not have access to an objective and ready-made ordered world of beings, prior to language. On the contrary, the world that we see around us, the common human world, is a cultural-linguistic construct that we have slowly evolved internally and amongst ourselves over thousands of years. Our history, our language, our theory and our form of consciousness all profoundly shape both what we see, and the way we see it.

So the world we see is a world that is through and through humanly-shaped and humanly-appropriated. As for the worlds of ants, whales and other animals, we have to see them as sub-worlds within the human world.

The human world has no beyond: there is no further world beyond this apparent common world of ours. There is no need to make any sort of distinction between appearance and reality, or between this lower world and a supposed Higher World. All this of ours that we see around us is all there is.

However, we are by no means the absolute creators of what we see. First, there is a circular, reciprocal relationship between the world of beings and the world of meaning, next to be explored. And secondly there is Being, the elusive no-thing, the O-Void, our M-Other from which every thing E-ventuates, just in time.

Perhaps it is just because it is post-metaphysical that our non-realist philosophy does not achieve, and does not attempt to achieve, completed internal systematic 'closure' without any remainder. We are as naturalistic, as anthropocentric and as language-centred as we can get, but *still* we find that there is a remainder, an ineffable no-thing, that resists assimilation. Being, our M/Other, the O/Void, our birth and our death.

8. The reciprocal production of being and meaning

Although many people greatly fear and dislike what they call 'reductionism', it is well known that natural science makes the best and steadiest progress when it sticks most closely to mathematics, mechanism and orthodox experimental method. In much the same way, philosophy makes the best and steadiest progress by sticking to sceptical questioning, clear language, and as reflexively-consistent a form of all-round naturalism as can be reached.

'Naturalism' here has two meanings. The first goes back at least to Spinoza. Philosophy needs to overcome all the traditional 'Platonic' disjunctions. It needs to resolve the old 'noumenal' world-above fully down into this lower world of ours, in such a way that we can write smoothly and easily across the old oppositions between form and matter, the *a priori* and the empirical, the real and the apparent, mind and body, and all the rest. Naturalism means that everything is contingent and everything is on one level, *exactly* as all the entries in the dictionary are interconnected and on one level. All things are in continuity, and interconnected in such a way that a single piece of writing can in principle roam everywhere without interruption or discomfort. When we have a fully naturalistic outlook we will see the world as our own world, and see ourselves as fitting perfectly easily into it. In a democratic world we see ourselves, Being and writing all as co-extensive and all as on one level, *plain*. To me, the thought of such a level, harmonious human world, without hierarchy or mystery, is beautiful, utterly beautiful.

In Platonism, reality was very violently and painfully split and hierarchized. As Plato himself makes clear, the idea was to create a scale of values, a social scale, and (above all) a cosmic background for the exercise of political power and control. Plato also makes no bones about the fact that he has made a world so disagreeable that the philosopher finds it best to spend his time thinking about death.

In our own day, our biological naturalism and our democratic politics make it urgently necessary to expunge the legacy of 'Platonism' from our language and our culture. In addition, we need to free our religion from the terroristic ideas of absolute power and control that have disfigured it for so long.

The second and much more recent meaning of 'naturalism' dates from the turn to language in twentieth-century thought. The philosophical text needs to become reflexively self-consistent. It needs to account for itself as text, saying where it has come from, what it is, and exactly how a mere chain of around 60,000 signs can get to be all about everything. As I have suggested elsewhere, the best way to do this is to overcome the traditional dualism between words and things. When we grasp the extent to which language and the empirical world are always already interwoven, we become better able to understand how a literary text, a mere string of conventional marks like these ones that are now before your eyes, is able to be a microcosm of everything.

Philosophy now, after Nietzsche and also after Heidegger, has then a dual agenda. Following in the main tradition of naturalism, it tries to overcome the oppositional and hierarchized 'power-structure' vision of the world that we have inherited from the past, and still find to a surprising extent written into our language. Philosophy aims to bring everything down on to one surface, creating a democratic and transactional vision of the world as a communications network, a continuous exchange of energies and meanings. The test of how far we have succeeded in creating this new vision of the world will be how far we can in a single text appropriate everything for everyone, writing easily across all the former barriers without changing level, and so removing all 'height', mystery and authority. Everything becomes a gift, free for all. This chain of signs, your field of view, your world, the world – it's all the same.

So: everything is to become easy, common, plain, wide-open, accessible and reciprocating. Since the 1960s there has been much debate about 'humanism' and 'anti-humanism', but I'd like to describe a world-view so fully *domesticated* by language, and so easy, gentle and unmysterious, that we are no longer particularly *bothered* about ourselves. Perhaps that is what science promises: all of reality gets to be so completely theorized by us and so well-wrapped-up in our language that we no longer feel alienated. Our own status in the scheme of things ceases to be a problem to us, and we can forget about it. And to the extent that we can become so at ease in the world that we are entirely happy to forget ourselves, we can also go along with the 'anti-humanism' of Heidegger's last period.

The rounding-off of this modern type of naturalism, then, requires a full interweaving of the worlds of being and of meaning. And why not? Consider, for example, how easily language moves both 'in our minds' and about the physical world. People who have taught, and have even believed in, a sharp mind-body dualism seem not to remark how easily our language moves across the frontier between the allegedly quite-distinct worlds of subjectivity and objectivity. The frontier is unguarded; indeed, one is hardly aware of having crossed it.

The worlds of being and meaning reciprocally presuppose each other and connect up circularly. *Meaning presupposes being*. Language requires a body or vehicle to ride upon or to modulate, and linguistic meaning (mean-ing) is temporal. So the world of linguistic meaning presupposes the temporal, bodily and energetic world of being. But at the same time, *Being presupposes meaning*. We never see, and could never actually *see*, a void, chaotic world. We always see a cosmos, a world already formed and made intelligible by our language. So the world of language is always already there, forming the empirical world; and the empirical world of being is always already there, sustaining language. Circularly, being and meaning continually sustain each other, just in time.[1]

Our sort of naturalism however does *not*, in the manner of Spinoza, add up to a lucidly-rational and self-existent totality. In the great circle of Spinoza's system all the definitions are supposed to be lucid and all the connections deductive. From the standpoint of the highest kind of knowledge everything is as it eternally must be: one is eternally happy when everything is rationally necessary. That is how it is for Spinoza; but that is not how it is with us. For us, everything is temporal and shifting, and everything is contingent, both in the realm of mean-ing and in the realm of be-ing. Each and every thing might have been otherwise. There are many languages, and many ways of world-building. *Our form of naturalism therefore can never claim to be more than a transient literary creation*, dependent upon metaphor, upon custom, and upon linguistic style; and always capable of a variety of readings.

From this it follows that our version of philosophical naturalism can never claim Spinoza's kind of completeness and dogmatic truth. We cannot erect an enduring and freestanding monument. We may (in theory, at least) be able to write a sweet and artistically-unified text that moves easily around the whole philosophical world and undoes all the old violent oppositions, whilst at the same time also explaining its own character as a text and its own production. But since what we are doing is only literary, entirely contingent and subject to change, there will always be something left over, a remainder, an outside, something we always presupposed and could not incorporate.

Being, with a capital-B, is the unthing (no-thing, pre-thing?) that we cannot quite include within our system – or rather, our work of art. It is always presupposed, and never quite *incorporated*, or 'embodied'.

The reciprocal production of being and meaning

Thus we push the end of metaphysics, radical humanism and the linguistic turn as hard as we can. We write a completely humanized world; and the more clearly and consistently we do this, the more clearly Being emerges as our hidden, presupposed Other, our source, our counter-part, our partner, our M-other.

To put it just a little malignantly: one tries to prove the existence of God by proving that naturalism and reductionism are wrong; but one 'shows the existence of Being' by proving that naturalism and reductionism are *right.*

9. Being's law

Consider for a moment what sort of being, or mode of existence, or degree of reality we should ascribe to each of the following familiar objects: a concerto, a weekend, a thought, an eclipse, a smile, a triangle, and a human right. Is there some stuff called 'being' that they are all made of, or is there some general feature like realness or objectivity that they may have in common; or is there at least some great cosmic plan or filing-system within which each of them has been assigned its due place?

At first glance the answer seems to be no, because the various objects seem to be so utterly incommensurable. None is straightforwardly a physical object, and although they all seem to be talked about as if they are realities, it is hard to see how we could ever hope to detect some common stuff running through them all and making them all in their various ways 'real'.

In the past the variety and disparity of the seemingly non-material real objects that we acknowledge has been taken as a challenge to philosophers, and from Plato to Meinong (and beyond) various attempts have been made to sort them all out and place them on some kind of scale of degrees of being.

Today, such ideas seem very old-fashioned, no doubt chiefly because of the influence of Wittgenstein. He argued that it is a mistake to try to work out a completely general and non-relative idea of existence or being or reality. In the many and varied contexts of life, as we play our language-games, we set up a great variety of topics of discourse, ascribing a kind of reality (or being, or existence, or objectivity) to each of them *within the context of the game to which it belongs*. Thus, when we are talking about mathematics we may speak of numbers as if they are mind-independent existing things with properties of their own; and when we are talking politics we may speak of human rights as if they are real things independent of us that need to be respected and not violated. But it doesn't follow that any univocal and cross-game common meaning of 'existence' or 'reality' is involved here, or should be looked for. Quite the contrary, for it is easy to demonstrate the absurdities that may result if we thoughtlessly transfer words and meanings from one game to another. For example, an explorer who makes a geographical discovery finds a new physical object, whereas a mathematician who makes a mathematical discovery finds a hitherto-unnoticed logical implication; and these are quite different sorts of discovery, which ought not to be confused. Again, we may speak of scientists as 'discovering' laws of nature. But we shouldn't suppose that one can either just bump into a law of nature, or find it written down in a cosmic statute-book.

So Wittgenstein stressed the heterogeneity of our language-games, and concluded that we should give up trying to formulate large and completely general statements in philosophy. It is enough to observe carefully how individual language-games are played, and what job is done in each case by playing them. It is a bad mistake to look for a universal meaning of being (or reality, or existence, or objectivity) that transcends all the games, and it is a mistake to try to construct a Scale of Being. We talk sense only when we stick within established language-games and abide by their conventions.

Wittgenstein's position may evidently be described as a form of pluralism and quietism. Is he to be read as flatly contradicting Heidegger? For Heidegger surely does seem to brandish the word 'Being' and to use it in a grand and global sense. Should we not then regard Heidegger as a prime example of someone who has committed precisely the sin that Wittgenstein warns against, and who has been punished appropriately by being found to write the most dismally obscure nonsense, just as Wittgenstein warned would happen?

Some of Wittgenstein's Anglo-Saxon admirers have indeed said that kind of thing about Heidegger. But here we should pause for a moment and see whether the teachings of the two philosophers may not after all be reconcilable.

Certainly Wittgenstein does argue that it is a mistake to go through all the very disparate objects that are posited in different ways in our various language-games, on the lookout for some universal stuff called 'being' or 'reality' in which they all participate in various ways. So Wittgenstein says, and he is surely right. We don't need to try to build a philosophers' super-universe, much larger and more complex than the physical universe described by the natural sciences, and locating within itself all the miscellany of objects that are postulated by mathematicians, moralists and the rest. But wait: there is something so obvious that we have overlooked it. Despite all Wittgenstein's stress upon the heterogeneity of our language-games there is after all one universal thing that does run through all of them, and within which all of our bizarrely-diverse menagerie of entities are constructed and posited, and that is *language itself*. It is we who let all the Being in, because it is we who posit all the entities and thereby open all the slots for Being to fill.

In the past, when people talked about ontology, they talked as if language were for them a transparent window upon the world. They tried to peer through it, attempting to see some universal stuff out there beyond language and of which all things are made. Or better: they thought of the Real as a *realm*, because all things that are in being are in comm-unity, inter-related and interacting. Language rightly used might be thought of as copying, representing or portraying the world of all things that are in being. Metaphysics might be a sort of descriptive cosmic *politics*, mapping the hierarchies, the laws and the constituents of the realm of the Real.

On this representationalist theory of knowledge a distinction has to be made between the world of beings, the world *in re*, out there, and the world in representation, the world turned into words, pictured in language. Reading a journalist's description of an event, one saw in one's mind's eye something like a *news-reel*. One pictured the scene: it was as if one was really there. The events were made vivid.

The metaphors we use in connection with all this are a strange jumble. They cannot be worked through clearly. 'A picture has held us captive', in Wittgenstein's phrase. But, of course, twentieth-century philosophy has been struggling to break away from representationalism, and Wittgenstein and Heidegger are not in the end so very far apart. Both want to escape from representationalism. We live in a single human world, the world of our language, and all kinds of being are posited and come forth within language. What things are is given by the way they are talked about, and in no other way. We do not have any direct access to things. We have access to things only through the language in which we speak about them.

In the older scheme there were two worlds. There was the Kingdom of the Real out there, the ready-made objective world. And there was the human copy of the world, which might be thought of either as a mental map or photograph inside our heads or as a description of the world in language. So there were two worlds: the Real World, and the human copy of it in mental images or in words. But in the newer scheme of things there is only one world. To grasp the change, slide the Real and the representation together. Now look at your visual field. See how your own feelings, your own ways of seeing, your concepts, your language, your education and social training are thoroughly interwoven with and constitutive of the scene you see. There is only one world, and it is before you. It is the human life-world, the world of *Dasein*, our perceived culturally-formed world. The way we see it lights it up, makes it bright and lets Be-ing come flooding in.

The end of the old two-level thinking, the end of representationalism, affects other sorts of object in the same way.
Suppose, for example, that you are interested in human rights.
Do you first read books about them, and then organize an
expedition to hunt for these objects and investigate them? Just
where does one go looking for a human right, and how can one
recognize one if one encounters it? And the answer to these
questions and puzzles is surely that it is a mistake to try to look
for human rights somewhere outside language. On the contrary,
the way to learn what human rights are is to listen to the discourse of those who claim them, those who argue energetically
about them, and perhaps those who recognize or concede them.
Human rights then come into being in language, and nowhere
else. You will not find them anywhere else. And so it is also with
all other things. The world of *Dasein* is not to be split into two
different levels, words and things. *Dasein* is linguistic all
through, so that Being comes to be always within language.
That's why research is done in *libraries*. Language is the house
of Being, and, instead of fancying that we play language-games
only in order to peer through them to another world, we should
learn to pay attention to the way we build our world by playing
our language-games.

Wittgenstein and Heidegger are thus not so very far apart.
But now a further question arises: a question about idealism.
Does anything constrain us? Might we be able to build any
world at all?

Consider: language does presuppose something. It presupposes Being. But B̶e̶i̶n̶g̶ under erasure, Being, is not a proper
word, not part of language and not clearly describable in language. I have described it as pure slipping contingency, even,
sweet, plastic and receptive to form. It is amoeboid; it may take
any form. It does not impose any restriction upon the way the
language-games may develop, or upon what may be conjured
up within them. Does it not follow, then, that we may build any
world we wish? Had our history run differently this past six
millennia, we might today find ourselves living in a quite dif-

ferent universe. Is that not so? Do we create our world *ad lib*, and out of nothing?

As Nietzsche has remarked, the people have always considered that philosophers are idle fantasists who believe nothing and think that life is but a dream. Folk are still saying such things about modern philosophy, and may ridicule us for suggesting that we are the makers of our world. However, it may well be that the very same people have always felt themselves to be able to understand without difficulty the standard doctrine that *God* at least is an anti-realist who builds the world *ad lib* and *ex nihilo*, using only performative utterances. God is all-powerful. Nothing constrains him, and just by speaking he can build any world whose specification is coherent. So the people who object most strongly to our suggestion that we ourselves may be in such a position are perhaps not philosophers who think we are talking nonsense, but religious conservatives who think we are talking blasphemy and trying to usurp the place of God. Perhaps it is because all belief in a ready-made world is implicitly theological that it is defended with such religious vehemence and tenacity.

The true position is as follows. I can build a little world of my own in a variety of ways, by dreaming, by fantasizing, by making a work of art, by writing a novel, or by building my own system of thought. In a certain sense, everyone builds and inhabits a little world of her own, with her own values, beliefs, and angle upon the common world. But the larger common world of our language itself, our language-games and our knowledge systems, is a very large and massively-strong social construction, built by accumulation over a very long period. It evolves, slowly, all the time. Everybody contributes a little to it. But only a very, very few individuals can hope to shift it much. It is almost entirely made of tradition, which is a huge body of accumulated 'case-law' – habits, customs, and done things. It has evolved in our social intercourse, it has been found convenient, and it has stuck. Often it is mythologized, and there are claims that it has all been given to us by the gods, or laid down by the Fathers, or even that it corresponds to the way things are out there. But no such ideas are needed today. For us it is enough to say that the human life-world, the world of *Dasein*, the world of our language-games, is all made of historically-evolved customs – customary ways of behaving, perceiving, speaking and so on. It is tolerably coherent, all contingent, and still slowly evolving. It is Being's law in the sense that it provides the given framework through which, for us, Being comes to be.[1]

There is an interesting corollary: any built and working human world can be a channel through which Being comes forth into beings and so – albeit obscurely – gives itself to us. And any moment in life, whether among the best times or among the worst, may be a moment in which we become aware of Being. So a full religious experience of Being is possible any-where, and at any time – even at the worst of times.

10. Being and technology

To a much greater degree than most people yet recognize, the great tradition of Western thought, the tradition that Heidegger calls 'Platonism' or 'metaphysics', was expressly designed to be and has always functioned as an ideological justification of social privilege and political authority. Philosophy has been a highly political subject. When members of the older generation taught Platonism to young people, they were teaching rising members of the ruling class how to feel good about themselves, how to uphold the highest 'standards', and how to rule with a clear conscience, in the sincere belief that they were selflessly devoting themselves to public service. So Platonism has always presented itself as lofty, idealistic, spiritual and generally in occupation of the high moral ground; and this self-image was not only politically highly advantageous, it was also deeply *sincere*.

The metaphysics of Platonism was a class metaphysics. It presented an oddly skewed and distorted picture of the human being in order to exalt reason above sense, and the contemplative (or theoretical) life above the active (or practical) life. Platonic education aimed to make people wise and fit to rule by disengaging them from the world of matter and the senses, training them in abstract thought, and making them into spectators of existence. So brain workers rank higher than manual workers, long-term considerations rank higher than short-term, and the 'pure' always ranks above the 'applied'.

All this has had a marked effect upon the theory of knowledge. In our tradition the whole realm of established and socially-authoritative knowledge has always been constructed as if from the standpoint of the leisured observer, the exact scholar, the collector, the gentleman-amateur, and (of course) the legislator. All our 'academic disciplines' were founded by such people. We still see our natural sciences in such terms, and in our universities – where there is always a pecking-order – broadly 'Platonic' value-scaling remains powerful to this day. We still maintain that the most reliable and authoritative sort of knowledge is knowledge of things as seen from the point of view of a detached observer, an impartial judge and a legislator – that is, from a ruling-class point of view. The worker is regarded as being too committed, too *attached* and too much driven by economic necessity to be a just judge of truth.

Post-Platonic ways of thinking about knowledge begin to appear around the time of the French Revolution, starting with Kant's doctrine of the primacy of practical reason. Various strands of thought combine: knowledge comes to be seen not just as giving rulers the right to rule but still more as changing the self, empowering and emancipating the individual who gains it. Enlightened individuals are seen as able to bring about progressive 'improvement' in many spheres, thereby increasing the wealth of nations. Steam-powered machinery vastly increases the productivity of manual workers, and in due course it comes to be thought that the manual worker who daily manipulates natural forces and materials is the person who is in the most effective and productive contact with reality. Around 1848–1851, the period between the Communist Manifesto and the Great Exhibition in the Crystal Palace, three new facts begin to strike British intellectuals: half of the population now live in the manufacturing towns, the new industrial working class is becoming a major political force, and it is becoming possible to imagine a future in which humans will inhabit an entirely man-made environment. During the second half of the nineteenth century a rapid social establishment of applied mathematics, natural science, engineering and technology gets under way.

Education, which for many centuries had been focussed upon the study of Letters, sacred and humane, now begins to be more concerned instead with equipping people to be economically active in a rapidly-developing science-based industrial society. Gradually the idea takes shape and becomes explicit that technological innovation is the single most powerful motor of historical change. Exactly *when* that idea is first clearly and persuasively put forward is not altogether easy to say, but perhaps we should be cautious and place it as late as the 1890s, associating it with the early writings of H. G. Wells and the later work of Ernest Renan.

The Darwinian revolution fitted neatly into this context. Only a century or two earlier serious writers had pictured the first human beings as contemplating the order of nature and working out for themselves and for the first time the Argument from Design for the existence, the wisdom and the goodness of God. After Darwin such a picture of human beginnings seemed comical. Our knowledge is not primarily speculative – or at least, it could not have begun in that way. We would never have evolved our cognitive abilities and our big energy-intensive brains unless they had practical survival-value. Our opposed thumb shows us to be *anatomically* tool-users. If early human beings were able to develop language, tools, social structure and a range of both technical and social skills, it was against the background of an urgent need to survive: they had to find food, drink and shelter, to escape dangers, and to get and raise their young. Inevitably, surely, the first human world-views were precisely *not* speculative or contemplative, but intensely practical. People learnt to see what they had reason to look out for.

Hence the shift in the late nineteenth century towards pragmatism in American philosophy, and in Europe towards the new philosophies of life and of action. We needed to get away from the notion of the human mind as a leisured, gentlemanly observer of the world, and learn instead to see our language and our knowledge as shaped from the bottom up by our practical needs, our fears, our hopes, our desires.[1] We are not at all disinterested or detached; on the contrary, we have a burning *interest* in life, and live in a continuous process of exchange with our environment, an exchange that is intensely symbolic and emotional, as well as chemical and biological.

All this makes it clear why Heidegger was correct in setting out from the first to write his philosophy of being in the form of a philosophy of 'situated' and *human* being, *Dasein*. Whatever capacity we may have for thinking ourselves into other possible viewpoints, our concrete situation is always *there* (*da*) within human Being's human world, seen from our human point of view and shaped by human needs and feelings.

Accordingly, Heidegger cannot be just anti-technological. On the contrary, we are bound to scan our environment, on the look-out for an enemy, a weapon, a storm, food, a sharp-edged flint tool, a mate and so on. We are bound to look at the world as living beings with an interest in life, searching for the tools and materials with which we can achieve our purposes. On any view, 'instrumental rationality' must always have been prominent in our make-up; and on any view human technical interests and activities have always been a channel through which Being gets formed into beings, producing reality, *our* reality.

In which case, *what went wrong?* In religious thought both ancient and modern there is a widespread suggestion that work is a punishment, and that technology begins only *after* the Fall of Man. In the Garden of Eden, it seems, there was no work, no tools or weapons, no hunt and no need to construct any shelter. Eve seems not to require even a comb. Our first parents look like gilded youth, well-nourished and good-looking, with all the requisites of life ready to hand and their bodies quite unmarked by toil. Technology begins with the divine curse that obliges Adam and his descendants to till the ground, and leads directly to murder when Cain uses (what was presumably) an agricultural tool as a weapon. The stories go on to associate technology with a lust for forbidden knowledge stolen from Heaven, and an insatiable desire for ever-greater power, which must end by attracting divine wrath. And what is surprising about the stories, in retrospect, is the extent to which, after all this time and after all that has happened, we today are still troubled by the same ancient fears and anxieties. One may well wonder why. Around the world the masses see that modern Western technology doubles average human life-expectancy and multiplies wealth a hundred-fold. Not surprisingly, they are struggling to get a share of it for themselves as quickly as possible. So why is that from Dostoyevsky to Baudrillard so very many modern Western intellectuals have been highly pessimistic about the cultural and religious effects upon us of our new technologies?

To judge by the all-too-abundant literature, this is not a subject about which it is easy to write good sense. Perhaps there is almost nothing interesting to be said about technology in general, except that we cannot survive without it. But during the past half-century a new global technological culture has been rapidly developing. It stores, retrieves, processes and transmits information in huge volumes and at very high speed. It contains a number of strands – economic and political, as well as scientific – and it is driven by a number of beliefs and assumptions that do need to be explicated. The point to be made is that these driving principles and assumptions are by no means exclusively or specifically technological: rather, they are embedded in and are characteristic of a whole cultural complex that is coming to rule our lives.

To illustrate the point, consider the close analogy and affinity between our two greatest tools of power, nowadays deeply interwoven with each other, namely *money* and *electricity*. They are, both of them, very precise, manageable, calculable and flexible forms of power. They have been created by abstraction, and are designed to be completely quantifiable, convertible, multipliable. Each promises in its own way to be the measure and vehicle of everything, and when they are yoked together the complex electromagnetism-money-information flows about the globe at the velocity of light.

The huge power of this new money/technology complex

does not stand alone. It calls for, *and it also facilitates*, an accompanying and equally spectacular growth in the bureaucratic supervision and regulation of life.

The point I am making must be clear: our new technology does not stand alone. It is part of, and thoroughly interwoven with, a whole new order which is at once administrative, economic, cultural and technical, and which is global and effectively compulsory. Its leading principles are old, but the peculiar force of their modern combination is very recent.

1. By technological advances, the efficiency and productivity of every operation is open to almost unlimited improvement.
2. By compounding the resulting gains, power can be used to create ever more and more of itself.
3. Resources like electricity and electromagnetic radiation and money are infinitely capable: with sufficient investment in research they can perform any task, make anything accessible and bring about any transformation.
4. Hooked into and skilled in operating the new information technologies, one participates in something that transcends the ordinary limits of space, time and contingency and begins to access almost unlimited possibilities of information and power.

Now, what do we make of this dream? It is the American dream: everybody has a right to everything. With enough effort and good will, every problem becomes in the end, as they say, 'No problem'. It is the old Godwinian and Enlightenment dream of human liberation by totalizing knowledge and by 'improvement'. Before that, it is also – it *was* also – a theological dream of salvation by participation in God's universal mastery over all space, time, knowledge and power. Before that, it was simply Platonism. With some specialist training one learns to abstract away from sensuous immediacy. One learns to access the universal intelligible world, and so becomes a philosopher-king, a spectator of all time and all existence.

In short, if we analyse backwards from today's ITutopianism, we recover in outline Heidegger's history of the West's forgetting of Being. Which gives us the clue to what has gone wrong. Earlier in the present argument the veiled assumption, which I have held back until now, was the assumption of Cartesian mathematical physics and of the technologies subsequently based on it that all qualitative differences can be reduced to quantitative differences. A complete description of reality can be given in the language of mathematics. Everything can be brought down to numbers – and then put into a computer. When that has been done, we have in principle the possibility of a complete and God-like knowledge and control of reality. Thus our newest technologies are still promising to bring the powers of Heaven down to earth, and to fulfil the Promethean dream by conquering time and space, ignorance and suffering. Everyone can and will have it all. Read about God's four-wheeled personal transport in Ezekiel (c.1), and then take a look in your own garage. We are indeed, and in some detail, acquiring powers that once belonged only to the gods; and the process looks set to continue *ad infinitum*. Indeed, some computer enthusiasts have already constructed fantasies along these lines, even claiming with quite unconscious irony that such a fantasy represents a fulfilment of the aims and hopes of orthodox Christian belief.[2]

Yes: our *techno*logical hopes are still *theo*logical, and the closer they get to fulfilment, the more they reveal what a power-fantasy our theology was. For when all qualitative difference is resolved into merely quantitative difference, everything is levelled, all values are destroyed, and all possibility of greatness is lost. In pursuit of the fantasy of participating in absolute greatness and perfection, we forgot Being and we lost everything.

This discussion has now shown why we insisted earlier that Being is in many ways the polar opposite of the old metaphysical God with his infinite attributes. Being is finite, Being is contingent, Being neither masters nor is masterable, Being is our silent invisible partner, Being is the giving by which we live,

Being is that which we cannot know or describe, but must let be and let go. But as we built and then pursued the dream of a total knowledge and control of reality – which we saw at first as belonging only to God, and then later began to seize for ourselves – as we pursued this ancient dream, so we forgot Being.[3] Strange, that it was a certain *fulfilment* of our old religious dreams that led us into today's worsening crisis of nihilism; and strange that it is so difficult now to find our way out of it.

11. Being and the end of thinking

In high-technology society the entire educational system gradually comes to be dominated by the requirements of technology. Vast numbers of people need to be trained to invent and to develop new technologies, to exploit them commercially, to manage them, and to operate them. Life comes to be dominated by 'instrumental' or 'technological' rationality, a means-end style of thinking that is engaged in an ironically end-*less* pursuit of ever-greater efficiency, wealth and power. But the more people are trained in this kind of thinking, and the more all of our economic life is dominated by it, the more we come to suppose that it is the only kind of thinking. Science itself becomes also only a means to the production of more new technologies. As for philosophical thinking, religious thinking, poetical thinking – most people have already become unable to perceive any place for them, or even to imagine either what they once were or what they might yet be.

All of culture comes to be dominated by technological rationality. It is all that is left of us. As we are, we come most near to behaving with the dignity of a rational agent when we are exercising the technical skill by which we gain our livelihood. But *this last remaining kind of thinking is precisely what our machines now do better than we do, and what we are rapidly handing over to them.* We are emptying ourselves out, busily delegating our remaining intellectual powers to the machines that are de-skilling us and making us redundant.

We are still very enthusiastic about this process. Around the

99

world 'raising standards in education' just means, 'making education itself into a technology that will serve the technology-system more efficiently'; which means, 'accelerating the process by which as the machines get ever-smarter human beings get dumber and dumber'. We are colluding energetically in our own intellectual expropriation, and we are not at all surprised by the fact that as the percentage of college graduates in the population goes up, so the general cultural level plummets. Of course it does. Dumbing-down is now the objective effect, and perhaps even the express purpose, of all our education. It seems that we actively seek the end of thinking. When we have handed *everything* over to our technologies, we'll be able to take it easy. *Ease* is what we were looking for: we want the machines to become so powerful and user-friendly that they not only do all our intellectual work and even take our decisions for us, but even thoughtfully relieve us of any need to understand how they actually work. Dumbing-down sells; dumbing-down is what the market wants, and what the technology-system therefore now works to achieve. It is doing very well. The economy keeps on growing, and human beings keep on shrinking.

In high-technology society, then, the 'objectification of mind' is now taking place with peculiar and final completeness, and the individual subjectively-conscious thinking human being is disappearing. Such people are no longer required. Only 'consumers' are needed, people whose ultimate aim is to become indolent passive lotus-eaters, sunbathing, playing golf, and just looking.

However, we must now inject a cautionary note, and begin to think historically about the objectification of mind. The reason for this, as we shall see, is that mind must always be objectified in some measure; but the form that the objectification takes, and the reasons for it, have varied historically.

What in ordinary language is spoken of as 'the mind' is still pretty much as René Descartes described it. It is an immaterial thinking thing, *res cogitans*, something whose essence is to think, an individual spiritual substance mysteriously linked to the brain. It has, it *is*, its own little inner world, and has its own unique angle upon the common public world. One of its capacities is that of representation; it builds within the inner world a model or representation of the outer world. But it has in addition a great range of other capacities and functions.

The Cartesian idea of mind is markedly individualistic. Minds – or at least, finite minds – do not overlap each other. Each is sealed up in a separate world of its own, and mind-stuff is quite different from matter. Cartesian minds, in a word, seem to be very lonely characters; but the Cartesian account of the mind has been hugely influential, and is still taken for granted by millions of people who have never read Descartes. So much is this the case that the obvious philosophical difficulties of the Cartesian account of mind are still today among the first philosophical questions that people ask. How can I know of the existence of other minds? How can I know that their private thoughts and feelings have for them the same 'colours' as my own have for me? And what am I? – that is, if I am always inside my own subjectivity and can never get sufficiently clear of it to compare it with anything else of the same general sort, how can I know just *what* my identity consists in; and how can I even *recognize* it?

Good questions: but they do not need to be answered. They need only to be taken as showing that the Cartesian account is radically wrong. No actual finite mind ever was, or ever could be, as sealed up in its own private world as Descartes pictures it being. A very substantial part of all human 'mental' life always did exist, and must exist, in socially objectified form. I behave intelligently – and can be recognized by others as behaving intelligently – only when I follow some publicly-recognized form, tradition, procedure, or pattern. There is always a code, and it is a code of visible *behaviour*. By using it I can make myself clear to others, and I must often use it to check whether I make sense even to myself. I am not content just to do the sum in my head: I *write it down*, to make sure I've not made an error. Nor do I just trust my memory: I *look it up*, to make sure I've got it right.

Thus a great deal of our 'mental' life and activity always has existed, and has *needed* to exist, in at-least-partly-objectified form. We often need to *think aloud*, for our own sakes, because the inner world of subjectivity is so wobbly and unstable. Knowledge also exists in objectified form when a social institution such as totemism establishes a living inventory of important features of the natural environment. Memory exists in objectified form when tribal traditions and genealogies are formally recited on ritual occasions. Standardly-used decorative, musical and dance patterns and rhythms may have profound cultural meaning.

This suggests a minimal historical sequence. In archaic times, 'mind' was largely objectified in ritual and in the Symbolic Order. People lived amongst gods and spirits. Then in literate societies a long process of internalization and 'mentalization' reached a climax in the spiritual individualism of early modern Europe. Consciousness was lonely. Out of its loneliness grew a need for liberation by knowledge, and for personal fulfilment; and now, at Stage 3, mind is disappearing again, by exteriorization into modern technology's flux of communication. The disappearance is set to be remarkably complete, and presumably permanent. We are already at the end of thinking. 'Man' has already died. Consciousness is redundant, and is vanishing. Nobody is complaining: people are happy to collaborate with the market research that improves the efficiency with which they are induced to play their assigned part in economic life. We help the system to exploit us, and so connive at our own elimination.

I have already described the end of thinking, and the end of 'Man', as coming about through the technological fulfilment of an ancient theological dream, the dream of a total knowledge and command of all things in Heaven and on Earth. The closer our technology gets to achieving a godlike surveillance, recording and optimizing management of all events, the more it makes us redundant. We become couch potatoes, lotus eaters. After all, that was what we wanted; but we suffer severely from loss of what is nowadays called 'self-worth'. All values are levelled. People's attention-span is already very short. Reality becomes only a flickering dance of words and images, with associations positive or negative. One doesn't argue a case for X any longer; one hires a publicist to improve X's image. Philosophy and religious thought have almost wholly ceased to exist, because their founding distinctions and basic vocabulary have been lost. As a result, people are increasingly unable to go beyond a crudely fundamentalist or 'dogmatic realist' understanding of either scientific theories or religious beliefs.

In a worsening crisis of nihilism and high-tech barbarism, what path should philosophical and religious thinking take? For a clue consider the parallel story of art. During the nineteenth century painting gradually detached itself from its traditional social function. Artists were no longer content simply to celebrate the existing social order and established beliefs, using the approved style and iconography. They sought to become independent of the powers that be, and began to practise a new and strikingly non-ideological kind of painting. After the First World War the revolt and the disillusionment become, in Dada, much more explicit and non-rational. This was a foretaste of a still more radical and sustained protest in the Conceptual Art that has been the dominant movement since 1970. How could one hope to remind people of Being in the all-out and terminally dumbed-down media society, except by administering a short sharp shock? So the artist becomes what in an earlier discussion (c.6 above, pp.56 ff.) we called a Trickster: a jester, a Shakespearean fool, a mad prophet like Ezekiel, or a cynic like Diogenes. When we confront a system that seems to fill the world and to define rationality on its own terms, we can't fight it head on. We have to behave in a way that is in its terms irrational, in order to draw attention to what it leaves out and can never wholly incorporate: the pure unmasterable slipping-away contingency of life, that which we always presuppose but can never grasp, the dark side of the Moon, the partner, Being.

In the 1980s I was described as, and much criticized for,

teaching that religious faith should now take a new form; it should be seen as a creative response to contingency.[1] But in reply to that criticism I suggest that although the pure contingency or transience of everything does indeed give many people the horrors, it is in fact what saves us. It prevents any system of knowledge or power from ever achieving final closure by becoming all-inclusive *absolutely*. It erodes away and gradually undermines the pretensions of the system. It requires us to make, do and mend. Ironical, is it not, that we are saved not by the incorruptible, but by corruption; and not by anything overmastering, but by Being's unmasterable elusiveness and contingency?

12. Human Being

Heidegger's theory of being has been described as 'ontological phenomenalism' – meaning that in his view there is only the one-level stream of purely-contingent events in time.[1] Everything just happens: no logical relations bind things or events together, and nothing *has* to be the way it is. His 'history of Being' involves Heidegger in rejecting all versions of the 'substance ontology' that since Plato has postulated unchanging metaphysical principles undergirding the flux of phenomena and holding everything together.

The 'substance ontology', also known as 'the metaphysics of presence', has taken many different forms: in Plato it is an order of intelligible essences, his world of Ideas; in Aristotle it is the primary substances, in Christian thought, God and the supernatural world; in Descartes, Thought and Extension, and so on. The crucial point is that the underlying and unchanging metaphysical order was seen not only as upholding everything, but still more, as supplying the ultimate and the only finally satisfying explanation *of* everything. After Leibniz it became quite common for people to argue that only an *ultimate* explanation can make us *completely* happy; that there must be a sufficient reason for everything; that we must look in the end to the metaphysical order for the intellectual satisfaction that we seek; and that therefore God must exist, and 'Platonism' must be true. The presumption is that we are entitled to expect the nature of things to 'satisfy' our reason. This theme has become so deeply engrained in our cultural tradition that when philosophy abandons metaphysics and says that there is only the stream of purely-contingent appearances, people feel that we are suddenly plunged into a crisis of nihilism and utter 'meaninglessness'.

What is attractive about Heidegger is the boldness of his attempt to overcome this negative and fearful reaction. We were quite wrong to rely so heavily upon the unseen metaphysical order to support and explain everything. The whole history of Western metaphysics from Plato to Nietzsche rested upon a mistake, and it was a very bad mistake. We were running away from time, finitude and contingency. We forsook Being and took refuge in dreams of absolute security, rational necessity, timelessness, and total knowledge and control. But now with the end of metaphysics, philosophy is at long last returned to its original and founding question, the question of Being. Now we see that everything that we had become so intensely attached to was an illusion that we needed to be liberated from. Just as in religion we come eventually to see that the entire doctrine system and the whole apparatus of institutional, mediated religion was developed as a protective screen to shelter us from the raw terror of the founding religious question, so too in philosophy the history of Western metaphysics in all its varied guises was developed as a screen to hide the raw terror of the question of Being – because of course the religious question and the question of Being were originally one and the same. Both in philosophy and in theology we in the West have for too long lived cocooned inside comforting illusions and we should be glad that a long historical process has at last stripped us of them. We now have a chance to grow up.

Thus Heidegger tries to persuade us that all our old long-cherished *solutions* to the great questions of life were in fact merely our *problems*. We needed to be rid of them, so that we could prepare ourselves for a fresh revelation of Being. And what form might that take? It must at least involve an un-shielded confrontation with the question of Being. So what *is* the question of Being? Heidegger (whether aware of it or not) in Jewish style turns this question back: Who's asking? And the reply is, inevitably, that the *human* being is the being for whom the question of Being is a question. And Heidegger goes on to speak of human beings as in a special relationship to Being. In our descriptions of what we find present-at-hand Being comes forth into beings; in our taking the ready-to-hand and making things we are ourselves bringing Being forth into beings; and the mystery of our own being, and of our relation to Being, confronts us uniquely with the question of Being. We are ourselves radically temporal beings, always projecting our own lives forward. Our understanding is temporal, our language is temporal and our activities are temporal; and Being therefore gives itself to us temporally, coming forward continuously out of absolute nothingness and into our life-world.

Despite all the radical secularization and rethinking that has taken place, Heidegger's idea of the relation of Man to Being still does a little resemble the relation of Christ the Eternal Son of God to God the Father, in Christian theology. The Father is an abyssal generative Fount, and the Son is eternally begotten to be his self-expression and his agent in creation. Being comes forth to manifest itself and begins to question itself in and through Man, just as God does in and through Christ. Man is 'Being's poem', very much as Christ is God's. But similar ideas crop up in other contexts, as for example when scientific writers express awe and wonderment at the fact that in man alone, so far as we know, the Universe has become conscious of itself, has begun to describe itself, to investigate its own laws, and to ask about its own beginnings. Inevitably some scientists toy with the idea that, just as colours aren't fully real until colour vision has evolved and sounds aren't noisy until hearing has evolved, so the Universe itself is not fully and intelligibly formed and real until it has evolved the being in whom it turns back upon itself and recognizes itself. As Heidegger puts it, when language comes it is as if an electric light has been switched on in a darkened room. Language comes and lights up beings. Until they have been described in language, the *outlines* of things are not clear.

Look up the *Shorter Oxford English Dictionary* definitions of the verb 'outline' and 'describe', and see there how the themes of graphic delineation and verbal sketching are interwoven – and quite difficult to keep clearly distinct. So the speculative scientist may very easily be attracted to the notion that the Universe itself at last becomes fully lit up, determinate and intelligible only in and through the scientists' description and theorizing of it. Indeed, a form of this idea actually figures in quantum mechanics.

Heidegger's theme of the special relationship between Being and Man is further developed when he goes on to distinguish between different modes of being, or different manners in which Being comes forth into beings. There is, first and foremost, being that *has* a world, and secondly there is being that is included *within* a world. This may seem at first like just another version of George Berkeley's division of beings into perceivers and things perceived ('spirits' and 'ideas', he calls them), but Heidegger's notion marks a big advance on Berkeley's. He is very clear that we don't just observe our world from outside, as if we peeped into it. On the contrary, human being is always already firmly situated within a world. It is *Dasein*, 'being-there'. We come forth into our world, and find ourselves *given* a world which is always an historically-evolved world, a cultural world, a furnished world, with beings present-at-hand and usable things ready-to-hand; and in our world our being is oriented towards the future and towards the fulfilment of our various hopes and goals.

From this it is clear that our human being in our world is comparable with Lady Macbeth's being in the play. She is not a substance, nor am I. She lives only within her world, which is the world of the play; and I live only within my world. She comes forth as a person only in and through the contribution she makes to the play, by the various things she says and does; and similarly I show up as a being, a person, within and through the web of meanings, interactions, and purposes that is my life in my world.

And that's all there is. Beyond that, being is Being – pure slipping contingency, abyssal, groundless, and in the Buddhist sense 'Empty'. Even the earlier Heidegger's outlook is already *both* radical humanist *and* anti-realist to a very high degree. Humanism and nihilism together – that is fascinating. In fact, it is thrilling. But more than that, this humanism is also historicist, for *Dasein* is not just the being of an individual human being, but rather, the whole human life-world: the world of the novelist, the historian, the dramatist, the politician. It is a world that is through and through linguistically-mediated, through and through social, and through and through temporal. It is the world of human action and interaction. But it is, in the Buddhist sense, Empty. It is ungrounded; nothing metaphysical undergirds it, supports or guides it. Which is why Heidegger can say *both* that his doctrine of Being is equivalent to the Buddhist doctrine of Emptiness or Nothingness, *and* that 'History is Being'.

A question now arises: within the world of ideas and the understanding of the human condition that we have been exploring, what is the relation between philosophy and religion? With Heidegger, and in debate with him, we may work out a philosophy of Being, an interpretation of the human situation along approximately his lines. But what *extra* moves are involved when we go on to talk about a *religious* response to Being and to the human condition as we have now come to understand it? Is religious writing something over and above philosophical writing – and if so, what? Does the *religion* of Being have anything *extra* to say; any fresh news?

Four principal answers to this question have been floated by the great philosophers of the past century. I have myself experimented with all of them at one time and another, but now wish to rule out three of them.

(i) The *first* answer is associated especially with Schopenhauer and the young Wittgenstein, and may be summed up in three sentences from the latter's *Tractatus*:

The feeling of the world as a limited whole is the mystical feeling.

For an answer which cannot be expressed the question too cannot be expressed.

(So, '*The riddle* does not exist'; but) There is indeed the inexpressible. This *shows* itself; it is the mystical.[2]

Wittgenstein has used traditional philosophical method to draw clearly and tightly the limits of the knowable, of thought, of descriptive language, of the world. This sounds very puritanical and very correct; but in knowledge as in morality, the more clearly and accurately the limits are defined, the more we start thinking about the possibility of transgressing them. So the young Wittgenstein's extreme logical puritanism sets in motion mystical aspiration after the Inexpressible that lies beyond the limits of what can be said. 'The mystical' is then a feeling for something that shows itself only indirectly and in an ineffable manner.

(ii) So we are told. But in fact there is nothing here to *aspire* after, nothing to justify the use of the word 'mystical', and nothing that has anything much to do with religion. If there is something here that seems enticing, it is so only in an objectionable way, as when in popular entertainment talk of 'the Unknown' is used to produce a frisson of excitement and to introduce a great deal of nonsense. Much more religious, and more interesting, is the move made by the later Wittgenstein when he returns us into the world of ordinariness, *Dasein*, gradually leading us to understand its outsidelessness and to be content with it. In which case the religious realm is no longer an ineffable extra, but is equated with ordinariness regained.[3] However, the later Wittgenstein does not only return us into the ordinariness of *Dasein* and leave it at that. He also has a doctrine about how we may continue to make some use of traditional religious language. Following Kant, he argues that we should now regard religious language and imagery purely as regulative or action-guiding, with no factual content. And this is the *second* possible answer to the question of how religion may still enter into our human being as modern philosophy conceives it. We retain at least something of religion as law – which means, as a set of rules associated with pictures that are to be entertained and used *as if*, or hypothetically. For example, the religious thought that 'God searches the heart' may be read as enjoining us to be honest with ourselves, open and sincere, and living *as if* there were One to whom all hearts are open, all desires known, and from whom no secrets are hid. In this way, we may still believe in God, but take a non-realistic view of God.

This doctrine of religious truth as regulative has a very long history, running back for example to 'the moral sense' of a text, and to the allegorical exegesis of late Antiquity. The Creed itself was called the *regula fidei*, the rule of faith, as if belief were indeed a *law*. But when proposed today as a formula for hanging on to one's religion in a secular world, it is open to very severe objections. It cannot be more than a temporary resting-place. It involves too much of an *émigration à l'intérieur*, and nostalgia for a lost religious world. And – perhaps most devastating – too much of the old imagery now grates uncomfortably. It has become morally unacceptable. Surely, no sensible person wishes actually to live under an all-knowing totalitarian theocratic government, so how can it be morally good for us to live as if we think that that is how things really are?

(iii) A *third* answer to the question of how something of religion may yet enter into the world of *Dasein* is Heidegger's own. In his later years, after the 'turn to the history of Being', Heidegger tended to present his philosophy as if it were a new theology. He has his own *Heilsgeschichte* (that is, his lengthy history of Fall and Redemption) and his own religious vocabulary of mission and destiny, giving and receiving, hiddenness and revelation, call and response, darkness and light, and so on. He seems to be mythicizing and personifying Being, in order to turn it into an acceptable substitute for the lost God. And this suggests that for Heidegger, as for Hegel and Nietzsche, religion is just philosophy for the people, philosophy decked out in anthropomorphizing metaphors. And why not? – For if the world of *Dasein* is as thoroughly human, social and languagey as Heidegger says it is, then of course its religious language is very likely to personify and mythicize. Indeed, it has been strongly and persuasively argued that the young Heidegger's secular existentialist account of the human condition in *Being and Time* is but a demythologized version of the Pauline account in the New Testament.[4] In which case it is scarcely surprising that theologians should have seized upon Heidegger's teaching with such enthusiasm, and not surprising either that old-man-Heidegger should be found warming himself up by putting on again the clothes that young-man-Heidegger took off thirty years earlier.

Very well, but Heidegger's doctrine of Being is so 'phenomenalist', so radically Empty, such a stream of pure slipping-away formless contingency, that he should never have reclothed it in language that might be taken to suggest a relaunch of the God of metaphysical theism. The only excuse that can be made is that so much of German theology since Kant and Hegel (and still more, since Nietzsche) had already become habitually dishonest in just the same way. Ever since Kant and Hegel, each notable thinker in the great tradition had known that the old metaphysical God, the superperson, the infinite spiritual substance, was dead. But they refrained from being explicit, and went on using traditional Lutheran religious language. (Some theologians are still doing this.) Heidegger in his old age, projecting religious vocabulary upon an almost-nihilistic doctrine of Being by way of gaining some personal comfort and rehabilitation, was doing something not very different from what had long been done by the friend of his youth Rudolf Bultmann, and by many, many others since the first edition of Schleiermacher's *Speeches on Religion* appeared in 1799.

Here we will say no more than that the elaborate cover-up on which Christian thought has been engaged since Kant cannot now continue. Instead we recapitulate the argument so far. If indeed the human situation is pretty much as described by the early Heidegger in *Being and Time*, and by the later Wittgenstein, and by the American pragmatists, in what way can religious language bear upon such a world and find a place in people's lives? We have so far considered and rejected (i) the completely non-cognitive mysticism of Schopenhauer and the young Wittgenstein; (ii) the doctrine of regulative truth, taught by Kant, Mansel and the later Wittgenstein, which allows us to keep the old language, provided that we use it purely regulatively as a guide to conduct; and (iii) the mysticism of the later Heidegger, which projects quasi-human qualities upon the Void in order to protect and comfort the people (and also, perhaps, oneself).

(iv) These three unsatisfactory answers being now set aside, we make instead a constructive proposal: we should turn away from theology as a distinct subject with its own special matter and methods, and instead see creative religious thought simply as a branch of philosophy. As such it is closely related to such topics as ethics, political theory, aesthetics and metaphysics, and it returns to the sort of status it had in Greek and Indian antiquity. Philosophers addressing religious questions in those days asked such questions as – What is Being, what is the world? What are we: how is it with us? How should we live? What is the highest good that we can hope for, and how can we attain it? In asking such questions, the philosophers were of course aware of the existence of many religious institutions in the society around them. But they were dissatisfied with the mythologies and the rituals of those institutions, and they sought to make a fresh start by working in a way independent of existing beliefs.

Our position now is very similar. For a very long period we have supposed 'religion' to be the name of a distinct and uniquely-authoritative sphere of life and social institution. It was concerned with humankind's relations with a higher world and as such had its own special subject-matter, body of truth, way of knowing, and institutions that guarded and policed truth. There were half-a-dozen or so major world culture-areas, each with its own distinctive religious tradition and vocabulary, such as Christendom, Islam, Hindustan, Indo-China and China, and theology was therefore a *regional* subject. The professional religious thinker/scholar worked within his local vocabulary, seeking to spell it out, systematize and defend it.

That situation has now come to an end. Huge improvements in travel and communications have intermingled the world's various cultural and religious traditions, making all of us as multicultural in our thinking as we now are in our food preferences, and the complex process of secularization has effectively resolved the formerly distinct religious world back down into its basis in our human cultures, languages and histories. Talk of a supposedly-distinct 'spiritual dimension', as contrasted with a 'material' realm, is still sometimes heard, but it no longer cuts the mustard. It has no meaning – which is to say that it does no real work in social life. Religion is ceasing to be a distinct sphere of life, and is becoming instead a way of relating oneself to Being – that is, to *this* contingent world and *this* transitory life.

Religion is now *applied* philosophy, 'edifying' philosophy, philosophy appropriated and lived. In the Anglo-Saxon world twentieth-century philosophy was mostly quite deliberately *non*-edifying. It sought to be cool, dry and professional, emulating the rigour of philosophical logic, natural science and mathematics. And no doubt there is a place for such aggressively-technical and non-edifying philosophy. But in an age of extreme religious sectarianism and irrationalism, there is also a great social need for edifying philosophy. It is time to tell the people the truth. Why not? They need it, and they are now ready for it.

This is how we might make the transition from writing the philosophy of Being to writing the religion of Being. There is indeed a special relationship between us humans and Being. Our human world, the world of Dasein, is the world of language. In it, Being comes forth into beings – which is to say, in effect, that the whole objective world becomes finished in our description of it and becomes conscious of itself in our knowledge of it. In a popular way, one might say: Yes, human scientific knowledge is the Universe's greatest achievement so far. The cosmos has through a very small bit of itself become aware of itself. But this achievement has been purchased at a price: we humans are aware, as no other animal is, of our own transience and our mortality. Much of our history has consisted of attempts to escape them. We have created vast protective ideologies of denial, as if we have found the obvious truth of our own situation quite unbearable, and have been willing to buy absolutely *anything* that promises to deliver us from it.

But when we write the religion of Being we use images and rhetorical devices to provoke a crisis. We want to bring about in the individual a full emotional appropriation of the philosophical doctrine. The shock is violent. It forces a break with consolatory illusions that are thousands of years old. The individual is forced into a naked confrontation with the *Seinsfrage*, the question of Being. One is devastated by Being's utter gratuitousness, emptiness, transience; its joyful solar affirmation even as it rushes into oblivion. All the idols are smashed, and amongst them such treasured abominations as 'what is mine' (including 'my soul'), 'belief', 'objective values;', 'life-after-death' and so on. The death of the self thus brought about by the *Seinsfrage* then leads unexpectedly to an extraordinary sense of deliverance and happiness, which has been described as 'ecstatic immanence'. It is a queer reverse-resurrection. One is raised from the death of illusory belief in another world, back into the truth of this world, now fully understood and accepted for the first time. It is a resurrection not into an imaginary other world after death, but back into this world, into 'glory'.

You will have observed a paradox: I have taught the Death of Man in two different senses. In technological culture the individual human being ends up as nothing but a passive consumer of entertainment – and therefore is dead. But I have also taught that the question of Being, when we finally wake up to it, *also* brings about the 'death' of the human self – albeit now in a fruitful and salvific way.

Perhaps in our present cultural condition the best strategy for the religious writer is to play upon and equivocate between these two different meanings of 'the death of Man', in the hope of converting the former into the latter: death-as-damnation into death-as-release-and-rebirth.

13. No object

I have been suggesting two theses that may seem to be a little at odds with each other. The first is that in the future the relation to Being may come to take the place in our lives that was formerly occupied by the relation to God. The second is that Being is non-metaphysical, non-objective and generally very different from God. The relation to God was, symbolically, the relation of a subject to an absolute Monarch, whereas our relation to Being is more like the relation of action to Time, or of a swimmer to water. Being is the continual temporal forthcomingness and 'presencing' of everything, our life's mater/matrix. Being is the outpouring of existence itself. Being gives itself to us as water gives itself to the hand of the swimmer.

Certainly it is the case that a number of gifted religious writers have written in such a way as to transform the relation to God into the relation to Being. Eckhart is perhaps the most vivid example.[1] But here our purpose is not to blur over but to emphasize the difference between God and Being, and to explain it. To that end, we must go a long way back, and begin at the beginning.

In the earliest stages of human life – in the very earliest times, in the simplest cultures, in the first months of life – the human being's chief task is to differentiate experience, which means that one must first of all define the frontier between the self and the not-self. Experience begins unselfconscious, amorphous, and very disorderly. The self and the world, subjectivity and objectivity, are not distinguished from each other. Only when

I have established the continuity of my skin all over the surface of my body can I possess my body as a unified and relatively stable system that is (more or less) under my control.[2] So the line between the self and the not-self gives us the body, selfhood and the first beginnings of consciousness. As for the not-self, it will take a long time for it to become world. Watch your baby hold its own feet, but pat the breast. The first bit of non-self to be singled out is the mother, the fellow-human. She is the beginning of the world, and through the contact of the mouth with the breast she is also the beginning of language. As Freud correctly perceived, orality is the beginning of love, sex and speech.

Against this background, we see why language was earlier described as moving over the surface between the self and the world, subjectivity and objectivity.[3] All cultures are much concerned to maintain the integrity – the 'purity', or ritual cleanness – of the body surface, because we give off and receive information not only at such specialized sites as the mouth, the ears, and the eyes, but also over the whole body, which is invested with symbolic meaning by clothing, jewellery, gestures, facial expressions, tattoos, scarification, cosmetics and so on. More of our senses than you may realize are not limited to specialized receptors, but are diffused over the whole body. This is obviously the case with the senses that make us aware of touch, pain, temperature, the position of the limbs, and the body's physiological state (for example, when climbing a hill). But the other senses *also* have a whole-body aspect. We respond to music not only with our ears, and to architecture not only with our eyes, but to each with our whole body. Thus music affects our pulse-rate, and architecture affects our muscle-tone and sense of balance. As our senses become more acute, we understand that vision is whole-body, hearing is whole-body and – I would add – language is whole-body. And these are considerations to be borne in mind when the body is metaphorically extended to larger structures, to social groups, to the Earth, and even to the cosmos.

No object

We see the sign, then, as a ripple moving over the body-surface. The inner surface, the underside, of language is the flickering play of the body's own forces, its drives, sensations and emotions. The outer surface, the upperside of the ripple, is the public meaning of the sign. In our social intercourse signs rub off one person and on to another, and the objective world is constructed out of that prodigiously-rapid trading of signs, back and forth, from body to body.

In summary, the world is constructed out of tiny ripples flickering over the surface of the body. Traded back and forth at very high speed, these ripples have acquired conventional symbolic meanings (think of the way you have learnt to read the tiny signals given off by your partner). So language moves over the body surface. On its underside or inner face we construct the world of our own subjectivity, or selfhood. On its upperside or outer face we construct the public and objective world.

A vital qualification needs to be added at this point. I am *not* saying that subjectivity is wholly made of nothing but private feelings and that objectivity is wholly made of nothing but general meanings. On the contrary there is, in both realms, collaboration between the public and the private sectors. In order to construct my self I have to introject public meanings so as to give form to my feelings, and in order to *put flesh upon the bones* of our world-picture, we have to project out our feelings. We put meanings into our guts, and emotions into our visual field. We interact physiologically with our perceived environs, and cognitively with our own innards. Once more: the inner world is made of introjected metaphors, and the outer world is plastered and painted all over with projected feelings.

This explains why it is that in every culture and in most philosophies the inner world and the outer world end up by being analogous to each other. The Microcosm and the Macrocosm reflect each other: the little world of the individual person is seen as having roughly the same degree and kind of political organization as the great world outside the self. And in the long history of culture the two worlds evolve in parallel.

They are after all made out of the same stream of language, and the same materials, namely feelings and meanings.

At this point we pause to observe that the story we have just told is not new. It is substantially the biography of the Winnebago trickster.[4] He starts life as a chaotic buffoon. He doesn't know who he is, or even what sex he is. His body is like a Richard Rogers building, with its internal organs on the outside. Frankly, he's a mess: at one point his left arm even picks a fight with his right arm and gets badly hurt by it. Only gradually, and through many reverses, does the trickster get his own body sorted out and under control. He learns about other people, and how to tell them apart from trees. So he becomes a functioning human person in the world.

We recall this fine myth – one of many such – only to make the point that the modern philosopher cannot pretend to do very much better than the Winnebago story-teller. The data are still the same; the medium, language, is still the same; and the story that needs to be told is still the same.

The politics of subjectivity and the politics of the cosmos, we were saying, evolve roughly in parallel. When the Trickster's body is an unorganized mess, so is his world, and the political unification of the body is a very slow process. The commonest arrangement has a plurality of gods and spirits in the cosmos, matched by a plurality of souls within the body. Thus the ancient Egyptian was traditionally held to worship seven hundred gods and to have seven souls. The full political unification of the cosmos under a single god, and of the body under the government of a single rational soul, was achieved only very late and after a fierce struggle. When? – I'd say: irregularly, and with varying degrees of clarity and completeness, between the Israelite prophets and Augustine.

By what methods and techniques might one strive to bring about the unification of the self and the world? By philosophical reflection? That tends to produce a rather too generalized, abstract and even *life*-less unity in both the self and the cosmos, as in Parmenides and Spinoza. By ascetical struggle? This notoriously produces a paradox: for if I set out to battle for self-mastery and self-control, I must proceed by identifying some elements and forces within myself as rebellious and threatening. I demonize them, battle against them and try to subjugate them; and I may succeed. But I cannot *fully* unify myself by this method, for even if I do succeed in binding the demons, they are still *there* and they may at some future date escape from their present captivity. In which case I will crash very badly. And certainly in our own biologically-minded age there is hardly anybody who seriously supposes that one should set out to achieve personal happiness by battling against one's own lower nature.

The third possible route to the political unification of the self is through monotheism. Here the cosmos is unified under the sovereignty of a transcendent Creator who is an infinite spiritual subject. He then calls the human self into being as his little counterpart, a finite spiritual substance made in his image, by him, for him. Thus the whole of reality is summed up in and subordinated to one personal relationship – which is infinitely unequal.

Here we pause a moment to say that God is real at least in this sense: that the idea of God is ultimate. We are talking about an infinite and eternal absolute spiritual dictatorship. Nothing more extreme, overwhelming and terrible ever has been or ever could be imagined by human beings. Only two things can be said in mitigation. *First*, the Jews, with amazing presumption, somehow found the strength to question and argue with God even as they were thinking him up. *Secondly*, it is not quite clear that any human being ever has grasped or could ever grasp the full weight of the idea of God without at once going insane. Since God, being infinite and omnipotent, at once annihilates all else, the thinking that tries to think God must be heading into its own annihilation as it thinks. To try to think God is to try to destroy yourself. In practice – and here we return to the first mitigating consideration – the Jewish response was wise. Just to survive, it was necessary from the first to argue with God, to struggle with God, and perhaps also to use religious practice not as a way of getting closer to God but as a way of keeping God at a safe distance. In the later development of the idea of God the leading thinkers always used – and had to use – devices for protecting themselves from its fierce *glare*.

That is all water under the bridge by now. Here, I shall say only that old-style realistic metaphysical theism is in any case no longer a live option. The religion of Being is different. It does not at all propose to unify everything around the one great theme of an infinitely unequal power-relationship. Metaphorically, Being is more like an unfailingly loyal, discreet and amenable partner. And if you have smiled at my metaphors, let me now in retrospect retort that the alternative was not funny at all.

The philosophical situation we now come to is very briefly as follows: we begin with language, found to be moving as if over an unbounded surface. The transcendental condition, prior to language, for language's actual movement is Being. Analysed, language is found to be a mix of two elements, biological feelings and cultural meanings. These two elements are combined in two different ways. Where biological feelings are formed by introjected and metaphorically-extended cultural meanings, we speak of the realm of subjectivity, the inner surface of language. Where a spread-out framework of cultural meanings is filled in and coloured up with projected biological feelings, we speak of the objective world on the outer surface of language. The surface over which language moves is the surface of the human body.

What stabilizes the objective world? The answer is that the world is stabilized by whatever stabilizes the meanings of words. And what is that? We learn the answer as we experience exogenous (that is, externally-prompted) jumps of feeling within our subjectivity. All the time different subjectivities are bumping into each other like dodgem cars, causing signs to rub off and be transferred from one to another. The bumping and rubbing smoothes and standardizes words, as pebbles are rubbed smooth by the sea. Thus it is social interaction that standardizes the meanings of words, and makes possible the building of a stable public world. As social interactions become more diverse and differentiated, the available vocabulary grows. A more complex external world can be built; and, by the introjection of metaphors, a more complex inner world of subjectivity can be constructed too. Always, the inner and outer worlds will be in some respects analogous; but that is not surprising when we consider that they are made of the same materials, combined in different ways.

The preferred order of exposition for our philosophy will run: Being, time, language, the surface, and it will then divide, between meanings filled with projected feelings on the upper face of the surface, and feelings formed by introjected, metaphorically-extended meanings on the underside of the surface. Social interaction will be seen as stabilizing the meanings of words, and therefore making world-building possible on the upper surface. In different regions social interaction is ritualized and disciplined in different ways and to different degrees, which accounts for the different character of the worlds built respectively by a scientist, a politician, an artist, and so forth.

So much for a quick summary. Here we note briefly that as we have developed it our philosophy has become much more languagey than Heidegger, much more biological and emotivist than Derrida, and (quite deliberately) much more pop than either.

Being is no object. Religion is therefore *objectless* or 'cosmic' love, worship, gratitude, joy and happiness. For example:

> As a mother watches over her child, willing to risk her own life to protect her only child, so with a boundless heart one should cherish all living beings, suffusing the whole world with unobstructed loving-kindness.[5]

The difference between 'profane' and 'sacred' love can now be sketched. Profane love singles out and fixes upon a single finite object. One loves this-and-not-that. Sacred love is universal and objectless. In a Buddhist culture one may say that *metta*, religious love, is love for 'all beings', unrestricted. In a theistic culture one may say that to love God is to love in a cosmic, objectless way. Paradoxically, in our own culture the decline of religion often produces a certain fetishism about religious ideas, so that a person may fancy that in loving God one directs loving feelings towards a mental image of a large, old, quasi-human person. But religious love for a finite object is idolatry. So, in practice, the metaphysical nontheist whose heart is filled with cosmic feelings of love and gratitude is likely to be the person whose love of God and thanksgiving to God are the most pure and uncorrupt.

In short, only the person who thinks that God does not exist can really know how to praise God, worship God, love God, and thank God aright. Provided that we put metaphysical nontheism first, the religion of Being may permit a certain reinstatement of language about God.

Perhaps we should in future write ~~God~~, under erasure, like ~~Being~~.

14. The way to Being

The discovery of childhood, the Romantic movement and the turn towards the senses and the emotions, towards this life and this world – all these factors have led us to value youth more than age, and to think that the best years of our lives come early on. The most beautiful and perfect human being is around seven to nine years old. It is possible to be very happy as a young adult, but soon we start to go slowly downhill. Women find themselves gradually becoming invisible; men begin to lose their eagerness. Life gradually turns into a rearguard action against the passage of time. We talk about preparing for what are euphemistically called 'the later years', but we prefer not to think about how wretched many people's last years are.

Is it possible now to turn all this around? Might we be able to rehabilitate in some form or other the old idea of life as a Way, a path, a pilgrimage, a journey, a progression or an ascent, in which a person may become steadily more blessed and happier right up to the end?

At first sight the answer would seem to be no, because various traditional devices and consolations are no longer available to us. From St Paul to George Herbert and beyond, the old theme of the Progress of the Soul usually depended upon mind-body dualism. While the body aged and sickened, the soul could shine ever more brightly: the two diverged as they grew closer to their respective destinations in the grave and in Heaven. 'Though our outward man perish, yet the inward man is renewed day by day', says St Paul.[1] But we have lost that sort of soul/body dualism, and we have lost utterly the belief that we will experience any *post mortem* conscious states. For each of us, the world is only as large and as long as one's own life. Furthermore, there has been in the past century a very large increase in our average life-expectancy without any corresponding improvement in our ability to postpone or overcome the many degenerative diseases of old age.

Thus the sombre truth, known to all of us even if still denied or disregarded by some, is that we have lost the old soul-body dualism, we have lost life after death, and we have only a moderate probability of a serene old age. So how can we hope to reinstate the old idea of life as a journey to blessedness?

We can do it. Both in Asia and in the Mediterranean world the spiritual journey was experienced as a journey from the Many to the One, and from complexity to ever-greater purity and simplicity. We keep all that, but also add a third theme which changes everything. The Way to Being is a gradual progression from the ontological 'heaviness' and 'thickness' in which most people live toward the extremest imaginable ontological *lightness*.[2] To most Westerners it will come as a complete surprise that this lightening or levitation – traditionally symbolized by the dance – can continue right up to and into death itself, and is blessed.

In what follows, please keep an open mind about the character of the progression, or series of stages, that is being described. It is not quite Plato's climb up the ladder of degrees of being and knowledge, because we no longer believe in such degrees; and in any case the Way to Being moves in the opposite direction, as we gradually learn to relax and drift free from the various burdensome disciplinary constructions of 'reality' within which much or most of human life is lived. We are talking of a movement into Emptiness: Being is levity or emptiness, whereas the thick ontology of 'practical commonsense' and the so-called 'real world' is the forgetting of Being.

The sequence we shall propose is not quite the same as either the classical Hindu sequence of stages of life or the Christian sequence of Purgative, Illuminative and Unitive Ways. We are speaking here of something a little different. It has to do with different perceptions of the relation between language, custom, the self and reality.

We propose, then, to describe the Way to Being in terms of a movement through five different worlds. They are as follows.

1. The world of pure language.
2. The epic world.
3. The human world.
4. The world of science.
5. The world of meditation.

Of these five the first and last are *de*constructions of the world, the former into a primal and disinhibited torrent of pure language, and the latter into, simply, Empty Being. The three principal constructions of the world centre upon (3), the world of ordinary life and human relationships. This is preceded by (2), the traditional world of myth and epic grand narrative out of which it developed, and followed by (4), the disengaged objective-knowledge construction of the world characteristic of science.

1. *The world of pure language* is the world of baby-talk (in America, 'parentese'), nonsense, delirium, dreams, madness and poetic frenzy. It is a deconstructed world in which there are no very clear lines between fact and fantasy, or between the inner and the outer. It is the most archaic of all worlds, well preserved in the mythologies of palaeolithic peoples, and in dreams and the Unconscious. Freud's *Interpretation of Dreams* is still the best introduction to it, but one may also learn a great deal from personal experience of madness, from reading such writers as Arthur Rimbaud, Edward Lear and Lewis Carroll, and from Grotesque, Symbolist and Surrealist art.

The world of pure language is violent, disorderly and torrential. It is very rude. It is the first and oldest world. Artists and creative people have to live especially close to it, but none of us is very far away from it. We draw upon it, because it *feeds* all the other worlds. It is the wellspring. It is the creative fount.

The influence of atomism and evolutionism in scientific theory leads many people to assume that the simple always comes first, and the complex gradually evolves from it. But an old and useful maxim in cultural studies advises us to proceed in the *opposite* direction: riotous complexity comes first, and simplicity is achieved only very gradually by a learnt and laborious disciplinary reduction of the complex, as in our writing we struggle to reduce obscurity to clarity.[3] So it is in this case: the chaotically disordered and complicated world of pure language comes first, and the various simpler and more rational constructions of the 'real' world are best treated as disciplinary reductions of it. They bring it under rule, divide it up, and simplify it.

When we look at the matter this way round we understand how and why it was that 'reality' was originally created as an effect of religious law, which imposed con-form-ity upon the disorderly excess of language. Religious law separated the inner world from the outer, male from female, the clean from the unclean, the heaven from the earth, man from beast, the wild from the tame, the commanded from the forbidden and so on. Sanity, and so reality, was in this way an effect of law, a disciplinary construction-by-reduction, a much-needed simplification of the originally overwhelming excess of the world of symbolic meaning.[4]

2. *The epic world*, the first 'real' world, is a grand-narrative world, divided into cosmic regions (the heavens, earth and the underworld; the wild and the domesticated) and populated not only by humans and animals but also by a mixed population of gods, spirits, demigods, heroes and monsters. Time originally moved in great cycles, but from the early Iron Age tends to become more historical, so that there comes into being a narrative account of cosmic history as a drama that moves through a series of acts, or dispensations, from its beginning to its end.

The epic world is often described in cosmological terms – as being, for example 'prescientific' and 'supernaturalist'. But to say *that* sort of thing is to miss the two most important points about it.

First, it is a very strongly *social* vision of the world, which gives to a large community of people their guiding myth and their sense of a common destiny. As such, the epic vision can still be very strong even today. Even in the twentieth century, it remained perfectly possible for such countries and peoples as the British, the Germans, the Soviet Union and the Americans to be at times gripped (whether for good or ill) by an epic sense of themselves and their own place in the scheme of things.

Secondly, in the epic vision Being is not yet fully given to Man, and the human self is therefore not yet unified, clear and empty. Humans still see themselves as surrounded by, and subject to the influence of, a variety of non-human Powers and purposes. There is much emphasis on duality and upon conflict – between humans and non-humans, between good and evil, and between the holy people and their enemies.

3. *The human world* is a world in which at last Being is completely given to Man, and Man to language – which means, in happy effect, that woman rules. It is the fundamentally *comic* world of ordinary language and everyday life, domestic, social and commercial. For some reason it is represented and celebrated most perfectly in English literature: *As You Like It, She Stoops to Conquer, Pride and Prejudice, The Importance of Being Ernest*. Why should the English, of all peoples, be so prodigiously good at the most caustic, comical and purest humanism?

Notice that in this construction of the world there is no interest in any supernatural order, nor in knowledge, nor in ideas, nor in history. There is only one topic – the construction within language of persons, their moral characters and the games they play as they negotiate and fence and scheme with each other in pursuit of their personal happiness. Which means that Jane Austen has already achieved the most thoroughgoing humanism possible, and explains why the philosopher Gilbert

Ryle, when asked if he ever read novels, replied that his custom was to read all six of them once a year. He meant simply the works of Jane Austen – which is highly funny if you ever saw Ryle, who in my recollection looked about as affable as the late William Burroughs did when he was feeling like death.

At this point the question naturally arises of how it ever came about that the tumbling, riotous world of pure language was ever successfully disciplined and reduced so as to produce the other worlds. Where did the necessary *force* come from, and who or what directed it?

The philosopher who first gave something like the correct answer was David Hume. Watch children inventing games and rules, watch your own body dropping into habits, watch new words becoming common currency, watch the process of *accustoming* taking place everywhere.⁵ In the relations between persons, in our relations between ourselves and our environment, and in our perceptions and our knowledge, we tend to cast about and seek, and then to drop into and make habitual, the easiest and most practically-effective way of doing everything. Then *the force of habit* gradually accumulates until it acquires *the force of law*, and may even become *sacred*.

So Hume's celebrated theory of causation comes down in the end to the realization that in this matter of world-building all connections began as, simply, convenient customs. The process of accustomization acts like that of natural selection: as in the biological realm the evolutionary process comes down to the action of natural selection upon random mutations, so in cultural evolution world-building and cultural development takes place by the accustomization and regularization of productive and powerful new metaphors thrown up by the whirling delirium of the world of pure language. Unexpected connections become insights, become customs, become conventions, become laws, which in turn may even become sacred obligations. And by this development of a body of rules a 'reality' is constituted.

A further inference needs now to be drawn. Our analysis requires us to draw a sharp distinction, and even a sharp contrast, between Being and reality. When realists set about urging upon us the claims of scientific realism, moral realism, theological realism and 'the real world', they are urging upon us in each case the claims of a body of rules, duties, obligations, responsibilities. 'Reality' is always a social-political construction, a lot of pressures, something that – so we are told – it is our duty to face up to and acknowledge. In English slang, 'the real world' turns out to be made of 'done things', local customs, 'ropes', mores. *Reality*, in the account I have been giving, is always an effect of tradition and of power. And all this explains why we use the same metaphors of solidity, heaviness and weight when we are speaking of reality that we use when we are speaking of onerous and burdensome duties and responsibilities.

Hence the seeming paradox that in order to learn to feel and respond to Being we should gradually free ourselves from 'reality'. In the now-almost-forgotten language of Christianity what I call 'reality' was termed 'the world', and what I have long called 'realism' was called 'worldliness', and was regarded as a threat to one's spiritual freedom. It was something conjured up by social habits, expectations and pressures, which do indeed have very great world-building power. And this helps to make intelligible the further paradox, that the largest and most powerful system of knowledge that human beings have yet produced, fully-developed modern natural science, owes its great size and strength to its strict communally-imposed professional discipline. Science, too, is a patriarchate. The world is seen in terms of closely-defined, standardized meaning and patterns. This is a world of universals, realist in the old Platonic sense, and rather markedly different from the human life-world just described, because it leaves out, even represses, the individual interest.

4. *The world of science*, the world of objective and organized knowledge, began to emerge out of its immediate predecessor, the Republic of Letters, during the later seventeenth century; but only during the early nineteenth century did it

become fully professionalized, and even yet there is some uncertainty about how in the longer term scientific knowledge and the scientific world-view are going to fit into the culture. If Nietzsche were alive today, he would surely criticize the overwhelming growth of scientific knowledge for the same reason that, in his own time, he questioned the overwhelming growth of historical knowledge: he would say that it is a distraction, and that it diminishes human beings. And he would doubtless refer to the fact that in the world's leading scientific country, where in every branch of science half the world's ablest people are working, a very large proportion – reportedly, a large *majority* – of the people believe in aliens, UFOs, ghosts and such like. Despite the high claims that many leading scientists make for the cultural value and importance of science, science in practice seems to do little or nothing for the culture of the population at large.

How can this be? The answer seems to have to do with the price that must be paid for the very rapid growth of, and the world-wide consensus promised by, scientific knowledge. The world is seen as from the point of view of a disengaged – almost bodiless and passionless – ideal observer, and is constructed in terms of strict standard definitions of words, of method, and of the ethics of knowledge. The individual scientist as a human being is required to be self-effacing and even somewhat repressed, in order to play her or his part in generating a body of knowledge that is impersonal, universal and ideologically neutral. Add to this the long association of science with warfare, and its constant need to make promises to the powerful in order to procure funding for itself, and it is not surprising that people at large see science as great for generating powerful technologies, creating wealth and winning wars, but as having little to do with helping the ordinary individual to win life's small battles day by day, to deal with the larger questions of life rationally, and to live well. Big science is great for big government, but does little for the little man.

Hence the anti-scientism of many modern philosophers,

including Heidegger, Derrida, and the even more pessimistic Baudrillard. For such writers the present, and still increasing, domination of the whole culture by science is the last worst stage in the long story of the forgetting of Being and the alienation of humanity from the world of symbolic meaning.

But it does not have to be like that. It is true that one side of science is indeed highly 'realistic', in the sense of being much concerned with its own social authority, and with questions of law and power. In Renaissance Italy the early anatomists were struggling for the right to describe and control the *human body*. In classical mechanics men like Galileo were battling against the Church for the control of *cosmology*, in all societies a key to the highest social authority: whilst at the same time in terrestrial mechanics the same theoretical work belonged to an old tradition of *military engineering and ballistics*. Against such a background, it is scarcely surprising that there should subsequently be in the scientific community a tradition of dogmatic realism, associated with strict professional discipline and with very strong claims to possess the most authoritative and useful knowledge in all matters of cosmology, medicine and military hardware.

However, there is also another side to science, traceable back to figures like Thomas Hobbes.[6] Here, the scientific vision of the world is seen as bringing to an end the old metaphysics of substance. There is no timeless world beyond this changing world, and no *Summum Bonum*. Living creatures like ourselves cannot enter, and should not aspire after, any state of absolute rest. Everything is radically temporal, everything is composed of moving energies, everything is in continual change.

In a word, Hobbes begins to make the move from eternal Being[7] to Be-ing, or Be(com)ing. He understands that the scientist-observer does not look at the world from a privileged standpoint outside it, but is himself part of and immersed in the same ceaseless flux that he observes and theorizes.

It is unfortunate that Hobbes' reputation as an atheist and a materialist has so far inhibited any recognition of the positive religious significance of his vision of the world. He is interpreted only in his relation to the Aristotelian natural philosophy that he is leaving behind. But it is possible to see him (and indeed also to see Lucretius[8]) as opening up the Way to Being. Both are naturalistic, both are contemplative, both see the world as in ceaseless motion, and both see themselves as immersed *in* the world that they think. On such a view, science might best be led *not* by the demand for objective knowledge and social authority, but by biology and aesthetic considerations. We might view the scientific attitude as a form of contemplative spirituality, contemplating transience, contemplating life, contemplating the Fountain. It could, like Buddhism and like Heidegger, teach us to look selflessly at the world and to let all beings be. Above all it could be solar, accepting our immersion and its own in the fleetingness of everything.

Indeed, a better and more humanly-enriching side of science already exists. It is well exemplified in the way Darwin studied and wrote natural history, and the way a host of biologists of the past forty years have studied animal behaviour. This work has shown that scientific work may be ethically and 'symbolically' enriching, and may one day come to fit easily into the culture generally.

I am suggesting, then, that the world of science is internally ambiguous, in ways that are reflected in controversies in the philosophy of science. Scientific realism first arose as a rival and a successor to the old theological realism of the Church of Rome, and took from theology the old totalizing dream of the union of supreme social authority, absolute knowledge and absolute power. And perhaps this was unavoidable: the Pope's claims were so great that he could only be beaten by being beaten *at his own game*. Science had to make the same sort of hyperbolic claims for its statements that the Pope made for *his*; and then it had to make a manifestly better fist of its self-justification than the Pope did. It succeeded, of course – but at a certain moral cost. Which is why we should argue for scientific as well as for theological non-realism. We should hope to see science in the future oriented not chiefly towards technology and domination, but towards aesthetic contemplation. Science should teach us to love life. It should make us happy to be empty, transient selves, lost in contemplation of an Empty universe. It should help us to be *solar*.

5. *The World of Meditation.* In his last, impossibly-obscure, writings and in particular in the 1951 lecture-course *Was Heisst Denken*, Heidegger was attempting to open up a new kind of thinking that would be a thinking of Being.[9] Heaven forbid that we should even attempt to follow his arguments, but one theme that does emerge is already familiar to us from Eastern thought: in much of our everyday thinking we think like hunters and trappers. We seek actively to capture, bind and impose a construction upon the flux of experience. We think so aggressively that we 'forget Being'. But the Way to Being requires us to learn to think in a different style, a style that is as mild, amenable, patient, attentive and receptive as Being itself. Heidegger admired Parmenides greatly, and he quotes the famous saying, fr.5:

For it is the same thing to think and to be[10]

or alternatively, in Kirk's version:

the same thing exists for thinking and for being.[11]

The interpretation I propose is this: when we learn to think in a way that is as mild and amenable as Being itself, we can hope to achieve a contemplative marriage – even a unity – of Be-ing and Think-ing. And that is beatitude. It is the religion of Being's version of the spiritual marriage, the vision of God, the Unitive State.

15. Being's poem

Being's poem, just begun, is man

I once asked the late Ernest Gellner, an interesting and courageous character, whether he held any religious beliefs. 'No', he replied, 'but I do have a religious attitude to life.'

I accepted that statement without demur. But if I could talk to him again I would please him by challenging him: 'Are you just reporting a psychological fact, or are you describing something really important to you? If the latter, tell me what "having a religious attitude to life" amounts to, why it matters, how it might be justified and what *difference* it makes. If having a religious attitude to life really matters to you, you can't just make a throwaway remark about it and then pass on. Tell me!' Gellner was always ready for an argument. I think I'd have got an instructive earful.

I shall not speak with Gellner again. But he pops up here to remind us that because the world is the same for all of us and life is the same for all of us, when philosophers begin to debate with each other they soon discover that it is very hard indeed to pin down the difference *in life* between belief and unbelief. Take a person who claims to 'believe in God', and then explains that what this amounts to in practice is 'treating life as a gift, to be received moment by moment as if from the hand of God', in the manner of Christian existentialism; or that it means having an attitude of cosmic or 'fundamental' trust, in the manner of Hans Küng.[1] Now take another person who says she doesn't believe in God, but instead 'loves life', seeks to 'live life to the full', 'takes life as it comes', and perhaps, Heideggerish, seeks to live in a trustful, responsive relationship to Being. What's the difference? Is there any?

Debating a version of this question in the eighteenth century, David Hume argued that 'the dispute concerning theism . . . is merely verbal'.[2] The world and our experience of life are the same for the theist and for the atheist. Each says: 'Look at it *this* way', but each under pressure will have to make concessions to the other.

The modern version of Hume's argument picks upon the formula: 'We should live in a trustful and responsive relationship to X', and then says: 'Just what difference does it make whether we substitute for X, 'God', or 'Life', or 'Being', or 'each moment as it comes'?

I agree that, today, it *doesn't* make much difference. And perhaps the conclusion to be drawn is that the more important distinction is the distinction between those with some kind of all-the-time religious attitude to things-as-a-whole, and those who are sharply anti-religious.

The religious person is a person who feels that none of us is, or can be, wholly autonomous, self-made and monarch of all he surveys. There is at least something there that one must *defer* to; something that supports us, something that we surf, something with which we are interwoven, something to be grateful to and for, something to be respected and even venerated. Human living is always highly *situated*: one shouldn't draw too sharp a line between the self and the world, nor declare the self autonomous. It isn't. We are never wholly alone. We are always embedded in and related to something we need to acknowledge.

By contrast, the anti-religious person says we should regard every injunction to defer to something or other as politically suspect. We should not bow the knee. It is better not to accept any antecedent limits to our freedom and our responsibility. In principle, one should be ready to treat anything and everything as corrigible or negotiable.

Thus the outlook of the younger Heidegger, as developed by

the younger Sartre, was anti-religious, for it led to a form of radical atheistic humanism which declares that we human beings do best to see ourselves as responsible for creating *everything*, including our own selves, our language, our values and our world. This was a kind of ultra-libertinism that refused to accept anything constraining, or even anything given, either externally or internally. In the celebrated lecture *Existentialism is a Humanism* (Paris, 1946) Sartre defended the old Cartesian way of beginning philosophy within human subjectivity – now conceived as a pure creative will.

Heidegger wanted to dissociate himself from this extreme and Promethean form of humanism and to show that he had 'turned'. So he replied with his *Letter on Humanism* .[3] The Descartes-and-Sartre type of humanism is still metaphysical, says Heidegger. It makes man a mini-god, a determined little world-ruling Will. But Heidegger's alternative picture replaces 'man' with *Dasein*, the whole realm of human Ek-sistence, which 'stands-out' into Being. That means, I think, that Heidegger's non-metaphysical account of our life makes us hollow, Empty, receptive to Being and willing to let be. We live in the clearing or 'lighting' of Being.

Evidently Heidegger wants to distance himself from Sartre's militantly anti-religious outlook. He wants to say that something is given and gives itself. Being precedes man: Being is given and gives itself. Further, there is also a certain sense in which language is given. We are not fully in control of it. It speaks us as much as we speak it; which may be taken to mean that just as we construct everything else within the language we use to describe it, so we are ourselves also constructed by our own language *en passant* as it flows into, through and out of us. So there is a sense in which language precedes man, and Being precedes man – which means there is indeed something (sort of) 'out there' for us to take up a religious attitude towards.

In which case the really-important difference at the end of the twentieth century is *not* between folk who think that there is a God out there and folk who think that there is not a God out there, *but rather*, between the kind of Sartrian for whom human beings are radically alone and who has no patience with any sort of religious attitude or feeling, and, on the other hand, people for whom there is something around us towards which a religious attitude is appropriate.

Very well: but *what*? God, Life, Being? Heidegger's teaching – here to be developed and varied – is that we should think in terms of a triangular relationship. The three are Being, Man and Language; and in poetry 'Man is Being's poem' equals: 'In the human realm the worlds of being and meaning meet, and catalyse each other.' We should not reify Being, and we should not reify language, but Heidegger undoubtedly wants to retain a place for religiousness in his outlook.

The suggestion is then that we should in future see religion as the pursuit of a certain harmony or equipoise between three principles: Being, Man and Language. Or it may be better to speak of a fruitful meeting of Being and Language in Man – a moment of creative joy. But before proceeding further we should paraphrase these three expressions. By *Being*, we understand be-ing or be(com)ing or Being – the continual forthcoming or e-ventuating of everything, which gives itself all the time. By *Man*, we don't just mean individual selves male and female, but the human realm, understood as the realm of human be-ing situated in the human world. We are always inside our own field of view, our own earshot, our own experience, and our own construction of the world. And thirdly, by *Language* we do not quite mean what a scientific linguist means. We mean to make a quite general philosophical point about the way the whole human world is pervaded and formed by the motion of language. We mean to draw attention to the medium in which this present discussion is taking place. And that includes ourselves. We are ourselves the products of the language we use: our world-building activity is also an activity of self-building.

The matter/form distinction, Derrida has said, 'opens philosophy'; and he's right. It is unavoidable. Being is to language approximately as matter to form. Being plus a certain knotting-together or condensation of linguistic meanings equals a being. The motion of language provides the slots into which Being comes forth. And, one may add, it is in 'Man' that the forthcoming of Being and the motion of meanings encounter each other, and the world of beings comes to be. Which gives us a rough indication of what Heidegger meant by describing Man as Being's poem. It is in the human realm – the world of human language and human consciousness (the world this sentence moves in, and that you are in, and I am in) – that the Universe becomes brightly-lit in all its fully-determined complexity, becomes conscious, knows itself. But we are not simply putting 'Man' in the place traditionally occupied by God. Rather, it is the meeting of Being and Language in 'Man' (= the human realm) that is Being's poem, the world as a work of art. And, one may say, the task of the theologian of the new religion of Being will be to get this account into proper balance. For us humans, the very highest happiness will be our occasional participation in this creative process through which everything comes to be.

Will the religion of Being be a religion of personal salvation? The old religions promised to the individual person an eternal life and a perfected selfhood. The religion of Being cannot promise that much. It promises only two things – aesthetic joy and happiness in death.

The reason why the religion of Being cannot make the old, grand promise to the self of personal immortality in a heavenly world is that we have lost the old, timeless heavenly world, and the human self has become insubstantial and secondary. This latter point deserves some further illustration.

There is not a single true self within you or within me. That is a hard saying, but here is an example. Someone who writes much may from time to time receive a letter that says: 'I address you by your first name because, having read several of your books, I feel I know you well. Now I would like to met you in the flesh, and discuss some of the issues you raise . . .' And so on. This correspondent supposes that the literary personality, the self in the texts, is the author's real personality. How could one answer such a letter? A truthful reply might run: 'I am very sorry to have to say that the person you feel you encountered in the texts is rather different from me (indeed, he represents a big improvement on me), and if you were to come and meet me, you might be very disappointed.' As I say, this is not an easy letter to write, because received ideas about honesty and truthfulness seem to imply that the self we present in our writing should be none other than our real and true self; and the correspondent may be deeply shocked and offended by the suggestion that the personality he thought was talking to him was a mere literary effect, an artefact, and something that exists only in the text.

I am not implying or saying here that the literary personality is nothing but a deception, a carefully-planned fiction. Not so. We don't in fact *plan* these things, and cannot do so.[4] It is not very easy to descry one's own literary personality, and it seems to develop willy-nilly, unplanned.

A parallel and non-literary case, to compare with the example of a literary personality, is that of the English music-hall entertainer Archie Leach, who by a chapter of accidents turned himself or was turned into a fantasy person, a post-modern facsimile of a gentleman, the film star Cary Grant. To millions, this fictional entity was of course entirely real, and wildly popular. 'Everybody wants to be Cary Grant', he commented: 'Even *I* want to be Cary Grant.'[5] And no doubt the writer just referred to similarly wants himself to be the reader-friendly literary personality that (so he is told) he presents in his writings.

The position seems to be, then, that human selves or *personae* are multiple, that each of them arises within the movement of language and/or other forms of expression such as piano-playing or painting, that one's personae are *not* very consciously planned and projected, and that they exist only within the process of their production.

So what *are* we to conclude of these various selves or

personae, whether fictioned or 'real'. How many are there, and what is their status? We can make a rough distinction here between (i) the literary personality, a phrase that we use to include the whole range of ways in which a self may be expressed in a body of work; (ii) the social personality; that is, the selves we present in our various social relationships; and (iii) subjective selfhood; that is, our subjective experience of being ourselves.

Of these three the last, subjective selfhood, is quite alarmingly disjointed and fragmentary: a wretched unhappy creature, and no sort of candidate for being the 'real' self. The second, the social personality, has more stability and continuity, and we may reasonably hope to find a measure of psychological stability and happiness in and through the maintenance of our family relationships and our work. Society provides us with small daily rituals and standard forms which give us a framework within which we can operate. As for the first, I am including under the head of the literary personality all the various ways in which through our work as a whole we try to make something of ourselves, to make our small public contribution, and to play our part in the whole show. And here I am suggesting that despite our best efforts we cannot clearly and consciously plan, or know, or control, or evaluate what we have done or what our contribution has amounted to. We can be happy that we have said our piece, and have expressed ourselves. But what we have said, what we have been, and what it has amounted to, we do not know and cannot know. There is nowhere where the Real Truth about us is laid up, and there will not come a day when it is made public.

So there is no real self, and we will never know what our life and our work amounted to. In which case, how can we be happy?

To this, I reply that we may yet have an extremely intense momentary happiness when, briefly, it all comes together and one knows one's self to be a scrap of Being's poetry. There is no one big overall Meaning-of-Everything – the world is too fat, bulging and shapeless – and there is therefore no state of unqualified and completely-secure final Beatitude. But there are still moments when, briefly, it all makes sense. Everything comes together, and we are at one with the making of the world. There are brief moments, but they are revelations of Being, they are moments of beatitude, and they make life worth while in spite of everything.

How do these moments arise? The only world there is is the world of *Dasein,* the world of your experience, your field of view, your body-surface, you-in-your-situation. This world is a world which has language, signs, scraps of meaning running about all over it all the time. Words swarm like flying insects over a trout-stream. They dance closer and closer to the surface. Dark shapes moving about below are tempted to break the surface, bursting out and snapping them up.

In some such way the dance of language occasionally produces an irresistibly potent concatenation of meanings, a powerfully unifying metaphor, a dazzling new idea. Being is tempted to come out and reveal itself. There is a violent stab of excitement. Because language links the inner and outer worlds, the very condensed art-idea unifies the self, unifies the objective world, and unifies the self with the world, *all at once.* That is what makes it salvific and blessed. For a moment we have glimpsed what human life could be like; the way things might be. There might be a world in which humans are not just technicians, cogs, but poets, creators, makers of meaning, midwives of Being. Religion, education and so forth ought to be organized to that end. But, of course, they are not. Perhaps one day they will be.

16. Faith in Being

Religion, like art, defies attempts to define it; but in antiquity the word was often used to describe a prescription, path or recipe by following which one could hope to attain the highest good – blessedness, salvation, release from suffering. Religion involved in the first place not *belief* but rather diligent *practice*, often as a member of a community of other people pursuing the same goal.

Theistic religion was religion that gave a completely theo-centric account of the religious quest. The way to happiness was by believing in God, obeying God, worshipping God, respond-ing to God's promptings, and so drawing ever closer to God. Theists usually say that one should be concerned first for God, with one's own beatitude taking second place; and this objective orientation of religion towards God makes the notion of *faith* prominent in theistic religion. Faith in the sense of personal trust in and obedience to a personal God comes to be seen as *itself* bringing one very close to God very quickly – so quickly that those who believe in salvation by faith may on occasion speak disparagingly of the older practice-religions which believe in salvation by 'works'.

Against this background, it scarcely needs saying that especially in Christian countries the theocentric and faith-centred understanding of religion eventually became so domi-nant that until recently it was widely assumed that all religion surely must be theocentric, and all 'faiths' must be *'creeds'*.

Against that background, the argument of this present book

has unavoidably seemed to suggest that the religion of the future will focus around Being, the question of Being and the human self's relation to Being, very much as in the past theistic religion has focussed around God. In Heidegger himself 'Man' has a special relationship to Being, rather as in ethical monotheism 'Man' is seen as having a special relationship to God. Thus Heidegger's own language suggests that God has somehow been replaced by or transformed into Being, and sets one wondering how far Being may be thought of as the object of *faith*.

How has the transition from God to Being come about? By the subtraction of the old metaphysics, and the old hierarchical construction of reality, from the idea of God. The idea of God was bound up with and sustained by a very large-scale cosmology. Remove all of that, and the core of religion contracts down to the relation of the human person to the pure gift of Be-ing in the present moment. One used to respond to an absolute, personal Creator: now one learns instead to respond to pure, contingent given-ness. I let it make me, and I try to make something of it.

As for the alleged 'special relationship' between Man and Being, we should note that it is not at all the same as the old special relationship between Man and God. In the old scheme of thought, a complex rank-ordered cosmos was already established *before* the creation of Man. With respect to his bodily being, Man was the highest-ranked member of the visible creation, and with respect to his immortal rational soul he was the lowest-ranked of the invisible creation. Under the Old Covenant in fact Man was a Warrant Officer Class 1 who ruled all the lower ranks, and was on the brink of admission to the Officers' Mess in the world above. Under the New Covenant, things got even better. From having been created a little lower than the angels, Man was by virtue of his union with Christ to be raised above the angels to the social summit. The redeemed human being would be like somebody married into royalty.

In the religion of Being all that elaborately ranked cosmology (Royals, officers and men: Divine Persons, spirits and visible creatures) has vanished. Our special relationship is therefore no longer a matter of having been chosen to occupy a unique position in the cosmic scheme of things. We know only our own mode of being, *Dasein*, our own point of view, our own world, and we have no notion of any other. I mean, we have no thought that there is or could be any other lit-up and language-formed cosmos than ours.

At last, at last – the metaphysical point I have been trying to make! Outsidelessness. The coincidence of humanism and nihilism. Anthropocentrism is, non-viciously, *all there is*. More exactly, anthropomonism in the religion of Being parallels 'christomonism' in Barth's theology. No language is spoken except the language that speaks us and our world. The world comes to be as lit-up, known world only in and for *Dasein*, the world of language, the human world. Look out of the window now: in your field of view, you see all there is – the meeting of Being and Language in Man. Us and all this, Be-ing away. This is It.

The point we are groping for here is abyssal. It can take years to grasp it. When we do grasp it, we are shattered. *This* is the hoped-for new revelation of Being: but perhaps it is not altogether new. *O pulchritudo, tam antiqua, tam nova!* So flexible is religious language, so much 'play' is there in it, that seeming anticipations of the religion of Being can easily be found by anyone familiar with the Christian tradition. Metaphorically, we have represented Being as more like a spouse than an absolute monarch wielding infinite knowledge and power; and this must surely recall the intimate eroticism of many theistic mystics. And I have also discussed elsewhere Meister Eckhart as an example of a Christian writer who quickly and expertly demythologizes the relation to God down into the relation to Being, or Life.[1]

More startling examples are available. The Anglican poet Samuel Taylor Coleridge, for example, is purportedly addressing 'a candidate for Holy Orders' when in 1820 he opens his Essay on Faith with these words:

Faith may be defined as = *Fidelity* to our own Being as far as such Being is not and cannot become an object of the sense. Hence by clear inference or implication to *Being* generally . . .[2]

Faith is fidelity *to Being generally*? It may seem that Coleridge is here explicitly writing the religion of Being. But of course that is not so: Coleridge is writing against the background of his own Anglican style of Christian Platonism, together with the more recent impact of the philosophy of Kant. Of course he holds that we are made by God, for God; and of course he sees faith in terms of readiness to obey the will of a personal God. And to that extent he teaches that the believer and the one believed in are numerically two, and therefore he teaches an heteronomous understanding of the religious life.

However, it can also be argued from the same traditional premises that Coleridge teaches, and is fully entitled to teach, an autonomous doctrine of the religious life, in which faith is seen as a matter of being true, not to another, but just to oneself. Our own supra-sensible nature is for Coleridge a moral nature, which lays unconditional moral obligations upon us. In obeying the dictates of conscience, then, we are being true to our own nature even while at the same time we are also obeying the commands of the God who made us; and Coleridge can therefore claim that Christian morality is a synthesis of autonomy and heteronomy.

Coleridge, then, is not as radical as his bare words might suggest. By 'Being' he means 'nature' – an interpretation of being that Heidegger (rightly) detests. And his – Coleridge's – present purpose is simply to find a form of words that will reconcile traditional moral heteronomy with the new Enlightenment and Kantian humanism. He wants to claim that a Christian who obeys God can still call himself a free man. If he had known of our present views, he might even have claimed that the Christian religion includes the religion of Being. And he might have claimed that in Christian theology faith in the sense of being true to one's own nature, and true to the nature of things generally, coincides with, or has the same connotation as, faith in the sense of trust in God and obedience to God's will.

But at the back of this little topic from Coleridge there is lurking an old and still-very-interesting question. Are the religious person and the religious object 'in' which one believes – are they numerically two, or numerically one? Are the self and God numerically two or one? If they are two, then faith is trust in another, namely God; but if they are one, then faith is that one should be true to oneself. *So which is it?*

Very roughly, throughout the history of the Abrahamic group of faiths the dominant view has been dualistic, but the mystics and certain philosophers have struggled to keep alive the non-dualist option; whereas in the Hindu tradition the non-dualist tradition of Sankara has always enjoyed at least parity of esteem with the dualism of Ramanuja.

So what of the religion of Being? In it, are the human self and Being numerically two, or one; and if they are two, can we speak of the relation of the self to Being as one of *faith*?

In reply to this question the first point to be made is that in Christianity both God and the self were, traditionally, substances. God was an infinite spiritual substance and the human soul, God's little counterpart, was a finite spiritual substance. The question when is whether we should think of the relation of the finite to the infinite as like the relation between a part and the whole of which it is part, in which case God and the soul are not two, but, ultimately one; or whether we should think of God and the soul as in apposition, and therefore as being numerically two. The latter view is the one regarded as orthodox by the highest authorities, who have traditionally, and understandably, rejected the notion that a human soul might become so oned with God – and therefore 'deified' – that it might no longer need to live in a state of subjection to authority.

What is the position in the religion of Being? Here, neither the self nor Being is a substance. The self is a mere collection of natural phenomena, fictioned into narrative or dramatic unity by the play of language as each of us tells the story of his or her life. As for Being, it is no-thing, outside language, Empty, contingent, gratuitous, unaccountable giving-ness, given-ness, transience. The self and Being are therefore neither two nor one. Being is not numerable at all, and the self's unity is only culturally imputed. It is not metaphysical.

What then happens to *faith*, in the religion of Being? The answer is: the same as what happens to worship, thanksgiving and other religious attitudes. They are all purified into universality and objectlessness. Our life is a gift, the purest gift of all, such a pure gift that there is no giver; and the appropriate religious response is a feeling of cosmic, universal and utterly objectless gratitude. Our worship is similarly transformed: everything is contingent, everything is transient, everything passes away into the whole, and we who are *solar* are happy to go along with that.[3] Our worship is the passionate, expressive and objectless love we feel as we burn, giving up and giving out.

For instruction in objectless joy, consult the passerine songbird in the Northern forests. During the winter, it gets within less than an hour of death every night: but at first light it wakes, finds food, and sings. How it sings! And consult the blue butterfly. The individual adult is very short-lived: it emerges, dries out its wings, mates furiously, sips a little, spreads in the sunshine, lays its eggs and dies, all in a very few days. But like the songbird it is bursting with the joy of life. And we, we who observe these creatures, we find that we are most profoundly moved by the most transient beauties: water, spray, rainbows, clouds, flying insects, birds, shadows, flowers, moments of love or friendship. Absolute, certainties and eternal verities leave us cold. We don't want to hear about them, because in the religion of Being the deepest religious feeling is evoked by the most fleeting phenomena.

In this context, what of *faith*, in a time when we no longer know how to believe upon authority, and when we no longer have the least desire to fly for comfort to obvious untruths?

Strangely, I still have faith, at least in the sense of being very ready to wait upon, to go along with, and to say Yes to the purely contingent, moment-by-moment, given-ness and giving-ness of everything. I still have faith in the sense of wanting to live purely affirmatively, without rejecting or denying anything. I still have faith in the sense of wanting to slow down and wait, wait, wait upon Being.

In the religion of Being, then, faith is no longer seen as an act of intellectual submission whereby we assent to untruths, under pressure from the community and its leaders. Faith is attention to Being, and the affirmation of Being.[4] Moreover, faith is acceptance of our peculiar human destiny as Being's Logos and Being's poem, bringing Being forth into symbolic expression.

Here we may draw a parallel with the old and interesting topic of the faith of Christ. God is an abyssal mystery, and Christ's faith is his acceptance of his destiny as the one in whom and through whom God comes forth into the human realm, in self-expression and self-revelation. Here, faith is something more like acceptance of the duties of a role, a vocation, a special relationship. One says: I can no other, this is my task, this is how I must live, this is how I want to live. That is interesting and very striking: the sense that a task in life is imposed upon us, and the sense that we have a special vocation, does come through – albeit subtly transformed – from the old religion to the new.

How have things changed? In the old religion, God had pre-destined, scripted, the whole story of your life in the minutest detail. During the course of your life day by day an unseen hand protected, guided, prompted and steered you so that willy-nilly you found yourself stumbling along precisely your foreordained path. Faith then was a bemused confidence that somehow, whatever happens, I'll make it, I'll come through, I'll get there.

Under the new order, things are rather different. Our lives are not pre-planned, and there is no hidden puppeteer pulling wires and managing the plot. Faith in Being feels subjectively very like an artistic vocation, or an addiction to writing. Creativity has become an habitual way of life. All day, every day, a bit of you is listening, waiting for *it* to *come*. But how does . . . 'it' . . . 'come'? It comes when the words that have been whirring in our heads all day, and the various forces struggling for expression within us, suddenly click together. Just for a moment, it all 'comes right', Being comes forth and there is a moment of creativity. That's *it*. That's what we live for – the moment when Meaning and Being meet, and something new is born. Our own personal struggle for wholeness in expression has met with Being's own forthcoming into expression. We are briefly one with Being, and we know what it is to be a son of God and an agent of Creation.

According to the Jewish Torah the prophet Moses once wished that all the Lord's people might be prophets. It is just possible that Martin Heidegger, imagining a future post-Christian and post-theistic religion of Being, imagined a world in which every human being is a son of God, like Christ. Being like Christ means being one in whom the abyssal mystery of Being comes forth into human language, and into the building and enrichment of the human world. An odd vocation. Nobody gave it to us. But it is just the way things are, language is, and we are. We are all of us, every one of us, world-builders, agents of creation, makers of meaning.

Inconclusion

People spend their lives looking for various things, but few seem to end up happy and at rest in the confident belief that they have actually found what they were seeking. For my part, I have spent the best of my health and most of my life in trying to reach and to state an outlook in philosophy and religion with which I could feel content. When I became a professional philosopher of religion in 1968 the quest inevitably began to turn into a literary project, which then after 1981 changed again into a *projet fleuve* – a journey without any forechosen destination. Now at last a long series of experiments in religious thought and writing seems to be reaching a sort of resolution and a paradoxical in-conclusion in the religion of Being.

Until 1981 I did believe that there was such a thing as getting it right by discovering the correct answer. I believed the journey had a destination, because I believed that there was an intelligible systematic order of things out there that might be successfully represented in a text. When I found it, I need only copy it down. But of course as I went first into non-realism, and then radicalized it into anti-realism and postmodernism, I had to give up that idea. It became apparent that the project was not a search for a ready-made Truth of Things, waiting out there for somebody to find it and put it into writing, but something more like an art-project. So it was during the later 1980s that I began to think of my task as a kind of artwork and to use the slogan: 'the truth is in the movement'. I no longer expected to discover a pre-existent and ready-made Answer that would satisfy me, and I wasn't even supposing that I could ever write a book that would satisfy me for long. Instead, I hoped that the movement itself, the course I was taking, might turn out to be the point.

My critics seized on this. 'There is no reason at all why we should take Don Cupitt's ideas seriously,' they said: 'He keeps changing them all the time.' Fair enough, from their realist point of view. They want only dogmatic 'closure' and timelessness: they want thought to come to rest in a system of fixed conclusions, the Truth. They will be completely happy only when thought has stopped forever. Meanwhile, in anticipation of that blessed time, they themselves have already stopped thinking. Lucky old them. But for me – as for philosophers as diverse as Hobbes and Derrida – we living, changing, *temporal* beings are bound to be rest-less. There is only 'life', and life never stops within experience. It never finds its own end or its own outside. And if all Being is temporal, rest-less and changing, there can be no fixed and ready-made Truth of things sitting out there and waiting to be discovered by us. As I realized the implications of this, I settled for the hope that it might be possible to achieve at least the sort of *unsystematic* truthfulness, both to oneself and to one's own times, that Kierkegaard sought. Truthfulness *ambulando*; truthfulness *in via*, on the way. I hoped that my intellectual wandering might seem in retrospect to have made a sort of sense, rather as a biographer sets out to make retrospective sense of a life seen in its historical context.

As things now look, my thinking has gone through five main stages, each of which was reached by radicalizing its predecessor.

The first stage, from 1967 to 1979, was dominated by *the negative theology* and the idea that the truth of theological statements is best understood as being simply 'regulative', or action-guiding. Theological statements don't so much *de*scribe as *pre*scribe: they tell us how we should think, how we should live. Radicalized, this doctrine then led to the second stage, the *non-realism* of the four books that were first published in the years 1980–1985. The non-realism was at first theological only, but was very soon generalized. This duly led me into the anti-realism and *postmodernism* of the four books that appeared during the years 1986–1989. I then faced the question of how it might be possible to go beyond, or escape from, postmodernism. The answer was the *expressionism*, or 'aestheticism', of the half-dozen books that appeared between 1990 and 1995. The religious life was seen as an art-like world-building expressive activity. We should live by those symbols that draw out and unify our feelings most productively. Religious truth is then therapeutic and aesthetic: we should judge it by the extent to which it liberates us to be creative and productive.

This was the furthest into anti-realism that it was possible to go, but in the end (i.e., 1994-5) I could see that a further change was taking place, *the turn to Being*. I had become perhaps too locked into my own terminology. Encountering Heidegger and employing some of his very craftily-chosen vocabulary might help me to be better understood: certainly it has helped me to come to a partial synthesis, or inconclusion. I am warned by m'learned friend that some people will see the turn to Being as a retractation; but it isn't. I can even claim that, as it has been presented in this book, it is in fact a clarifying restatement of the position that was earlier set out in *The Time Being* (1992)[1] and *The Last Philosophy* (1995a). The religion of Being is, I hope, interestingly intermediate between theism and Buddhism, East and West, Eternal Being and Absolute Nothingness. And, as I have been at pains to show, Being is not patriarchal in the way that God always is. Being, our M-Other, the O-Void, is receptive to female imagery. In my philosophy the deep affinity and analogy between the microcosm and the Macrocosm makes a measure of anthropomorphism perfectly acceptable. It is built-in, and is recognized for what it is. Further, I describe the exaltation of God, the forgetting of Being, and the subsequent horror of nihilism as having been – in part at least – ideological expressions of the subjection of women. In the religion of Being, Woman comes back.

However, I cannot claim to be any sort of expert upon my own ideas. When they have been coming with most force they have caused me such violent elation and distress that I could not clearly and calmly understand them, nor bear to speak about them except some years in arrears. Indeed, I used to have to warn hosts that I would speak and could only speak about where I was two or three years ago! However, the simple schema I have just described is indicated in the Introductions to the various books, and it is what, rightly or wrongly, I seemed to myself to be up to at the time. But other and wiser heads than mine may one day give better accounts of what I was doing, if indeed the journey I have made is ever thought worth studying by others.

As I look back now, it seems to me that I have almost been on rails. What seemed at the time to be a disorderly rush looks in retrospect like a steady movement through five stages of radicalization of 'Mansel's Theory of Regulative Truth' (1967),[2] following an almost Hegelian logic of development away from metaphysics and towards a position somewhere between pragmatism, aestheticism and Buddhism.

Is that what has happened? I don't know. And why did I start where I did, with the Negative Theology and the notion that theological statements are rightly understood as being not speculative but practical or 'regulative'? I had no idea, when I began, of where these two impeccably orthodox and traditional theological principles might lead me. But why did I adopt them?

To this the answer may be that the human race is divided into adders and subtractors – and I'm a subtractor. When asked how to improve the look of any place or system of ideas, adders at once think of embellishing it by putting in something extra, well to the fore. Subtractors think first of removing the eyesores: they seek to strengthen things by purging and purifying them. In theology, adders follow the *via affirmativa*, the Way of Affirmation of the Images, whereas subtractors follow the *via negativa*, the Way of Negation. Radicalized, the affirmative (or 'kataphatic') way leads eventually to the view that everything is

God, everything is eternal, and ultimately to Spinoza's block-universe.[3] By contrast, the negative (or 'apophatic') way leads eventually to the view that Nothing is God, nothing is eternal, and to an experience of God indistinguishable from the blissful void of Buddhism. When everything that is not-God has been unthought, one is left suspended in an Empty Infinite. In mysticism, we subtractors like the simple prescription of St John of the Cross: *Nada, nada, nada, nada, nada*, a five-fold *nothing*. In nothingness, we've nothing to fear. When I am inwardly coolest and emptiest, I am happiest. The less the better.

Since I ended up thinking that everything is contingent, the fact that I happened to be a subtractor must itself also be nothing special, but just another contingent fact. It is, then, just a psychological fact that I have, or had, a monkish and minimalist streak in me. But now I'm finding it harder to find out what to blame for my five-stage rake's progress from the high orthodoxy of the old Negative Way to the religion of Being. Was there, or was there not, some sort of necessity or fatality that drove me along the path I took?

I'm not sure. Heidegger himself took a somewhat similar path. Of conservative and modest south-west-German Catholic origins, he seems to have thought at first of becoming a priest, and then a Jesuit, and later to have had ideas of securing a chair teaching the history of medieval philosophy in a Catholic institution. It did not work out. He broke with the Church (but not expressly with Christianity) over its habitual use of law to control truth, and he ended up thinking of but never actually elaborating the religion of Being. Do we *have* to take the path that in retrospect we find we've come by?

The question much resembles one that arises in relation to biological evolution, and especially to what we used to call 'orthogenesis' – development in what seems to have been a straight line,[4] towards what people call 'the logical conclusion' of a particular course or sequence. Perhaps here the appearance of necessity is statistical: if the number of contingencies coming forward all the time is large enough, the process of selection will tend to create an appearance of orderly, logical development. Does something like that happen in our thinking, over the long years?

I suspect so; I suspect that we are talking here of psychological rather than logical necessitation, and of statistical probabilities rather than strict implications. But one way to find the answer might be to ask you whether you can work out what the next station along the line will be, if it were to happen that you or someone else were to take up the baton and continue the project. I plant the suggestion, not only to torment you, but also in order to subvert this book. You mustn't suppose that my conclusion is *the* conclusion. We really *do* have to give up the idea of stable, fixed and objective truth. And that is a good inconclusion to end with: I don't fully understand why I have come to the place where I am now. But I'm happy – for now.

*   *   *

For twenty years now I have been trying to suggest that innovative and experimental religious thinking and practice are possible, can be democratized, and are intensely exciting and valuable. Indeed, the books were intended to be themselves specimens of the new kind of post-dogmatic religious thinking that they commended. Old thinking will not do any longer; new ways of thinking need to be invented. I wanted to suggest that a good world would be a world in which *everyone* is religiously productive. We need to invent a vocabulary for such a world.

The notion that religious creativity can and should be democratized is now new. Moses has it: 'Would that all the LORD's people were prophets, that the LORD would put his spirit upon them!',[5] he declares. Like many other faiths, Christianity recalls a powerful democratic impulse at its beginning, that – so it is hoped – will return after its historical end. Might that be about . . . *now*?

Unfortunately, it seems that the only group that has achieved and has successfully clung to religious democracy within history has been the Society of Friends. Everyone else has given it up, pushing it away into a past Golden Age or an ideal future. Why is this? Perhaps because creative living, living by the religious imagination, is such hard work and so stressful. After a while, as the temperature cools, people drop back into living by rote – living by customs, routines and laws, and living vicariously. One can hardly blame them, if one has experienced the alarmingly extreme elation and anxiety that usually accompanies creative work. One understands only too well why Wittgenstein urged his pupils to give up philosophy and do something saner – like working in a shop – instead.

I'm worried here about my own motives. Why am I urging the joys of a way of life that very often proves psychologically destructive? Many of the creative people I have most admired – people like Pascal, Kierkegaard, and Nietzsche – cracked up in their forties; but instead of being warned by their example I followed it, and have in effect been urging others to repeat my own mistake. Why?

Again, I don't know: but I hope that the religion of Being offers the possibility of a calmer, easier kind of religious thinking in the future. I now want to slow down into it myself, and I hope that in a new generation there will be people who are less scarred than I am by the extreme ideological violence of our past, people to whom the new kind of thinking will come easily. Perhaps, perhaps, the worst is now over. I hope so.

*   *   *

All societies are protective towards their traditional beliefs, values and symbols of 'identity', but as we approach the turn of the millennium I wonder how long Christians can continue to live in a state of impotent, nostalgic half-belief. Any theologian who attempts to innovate and experiment in matters of faith encounters the most virulent hostility from people who do not themselves hold the core-group of ancient supernatural beliefs that he is questioning; but they think the theologian *should* hold them, and they hate him for saying openly what everybody thinks privately.

I have met this oddly contradictory attitude throughout the past twenty years, and most frequently from professional philosophers, from post-Christian journalists and religious commentators, from senior churchmen and even from reputedly 'liberal' theologians. Every single one of these people knows the score: they know that 'the Faith' that is embodied in our major religious institutions stopped developing at some time in the early seventeenth century. They know that the old beliefs have crumbled under the impact successively of philosophical criticism, historical criticism, developing scientific knowledge, and political and social change. They know that what used to be believed because it was rationally judged to be true has gradually retreated into worse and worse fideism, authoritarianism and traditionalism, and is now terminally sick. They are not believers themselves: but they want certain other people to go on believing *for* them, and somehow they are still not ready to permit the truth to be told publicly. They want a pretence to be kept up – by others.

Their attitude is well illustrated by an event that took place in 1991. I was in Australia. An archbishop there took the opportunity to denounce me and my ideas at a big church gathering. Afterwards, one of his cathedral clergy asked him why he had done this. 'Well,' replied the prelate reasonably: 'Privately, I've got a lot of sympathy for his ideas. But you can't *say* so, can you?' – meaning that the leaders of the community cannot risk disturbing the faith of the common people, and cannot appear to be questioning openly myths to which they personally are committed *ex officio*. In the same way the Chief Rabbi still declares in public that a Jew is committed to the belief that God dictated the entire Torah in Hebrew to Moses. That is what you have to say: as every religious leader knows, untruth is obligatory for the sake of the people.

The philosophers' version of this idea, from Plato to Leo

Strauss, is that philosophy cannot and should not be democratized. Truth is for the élite only: the people will always need
religion, and the wise philosopher will not dream of tampering
with their faith. On the contrary, he will actively protect it.
Plato even found time to design a religion suitable for the
common people, and there are a few professional philosophers
and conservative theorists today who take Plato's view. The
Noble Lie must go on being told, for the sake of public order
and continuity with our past, and it is the job of theologians to
tell it.

In reply, I say that even if this line were at one time
defensible, it cannot be peddled for ever. By now we have
had too many centuries of slow decline and half-belief. Is it
seriously supposed that in the third millennium we can continue
to teach a fifteenth- or sixteenth-century world-view to the
people with conviction? We wouldn't treat the sick according to
the prescriptions of sixteenth-century medicine, so how can we
suppose that in the far greater and more important matter of
religion sixteenth-century prescriptions will remain adequate?

In reply to this last question, it seems to be widely supposed
that religious beliefs are immutable fixtures. They are just *there*,
and they cannot be modified. You either accept them or reject
them, and that's that. To people who think like this, the very
idea that there could be such a thing as creative and innovative
religious thought is bewildering. They are just as much confused
and offended by modern religious thought as they are by
'Modern Art'.

It's a tough climate. But the artists struggled courageously on
in the teeth of adversity until, gradually, the point of what they
were doing began to sink in. In philosophy and in religious
thought we'll have to follow their example, and hope that
eventually people will begin to see what we are up to. I am
tickled by the thought that, just as ordinary people who are
medically in dire straits make great efforts to gain access to the
latest medical treatments, so one day there may be people who
take religion with such intellectual seriousness that they will

rush to avail themselves of the latest thing in religious thought. Now, *that*'ll be the day.

* * *

It is well know that Heidegger's thought is heavily influenced by Christianity, both Catholic and Protestant. *Being and Time* transcribes the Pauline doctrine of man and the human condition, and was enthusiastically seized upon by both Christian and atheistic existentialism. Less often noticed, but even more striking, is the extent to which Heidegger's later thought secularizes or immanentizes themes from the old Christian dogmatic theology. Thus, while insisting that Being is not God, I have noted that there is an analogy of proportionality:

God : Christ : : Being : Man

Man is Being's poem, as Christ is God's Son or Word. And there is even a striking Trinitarian analogy:

Father : Son : Holy Spirit : : Being : Man : Language

– which is worth reflecting about in some detail.

Heidegger really does secularize: we are to remember that Being, man and language are all of them finite, contingent, temporal. But I have suggested that when, in meditation upon what is before us in our own visual field, we suddenly grasp their aseity and outsideless unity, we may experience a sudden flood of unparalleled religious happiness. It is the new, secular version of the Vision of God, and it is overwhelming.

The religion of Being is thus the completest secularization of Christianity, globalized, freed of patriarchy, and compatible now with Buddhism.

* * *

An advisor instructs me to state very briefly the political and ecclesiological views to which I have been led. For many years I have put language first. One cannot any longer *write*, with reflexive self-consistency, on any other basis. Accordingly, I have held that everything – the sum of all meanings and truths, all realities and values – is produced within and by the common conversation of humanity. Anthropomonism, I once called it; and it is a highly democratic vision of the world: everything depends upon, and is held steady within, the ceaseless to-and-fro of human communication, human interaction, human trade. In which case the best world is surely the most democratic: in principle, everyone needs to have a say. Everything is negotiated and everything is in principle renegotiable. Conversation and accumulated custom produce everything, and as time goes by they also continuously amend and revise everything.

Language is in constant motion. Everything shifts and the rules of the game evolve all the time. So it comes about that what used to be called 'the popular sanction' turns out to be sufficient. Each of us needs to understand others and also needs to make himself or herself understood. Our common interest in successful communication is strong enough, both to build the world and hold it steady, and also at the same time to keep language alive and in motion so that the world can slowly change.

We do not need to follow those enthusiastic Maoists who used to insist upon a lengthy mass meeting each morning to agree all the rules for the day ahead. Human social life already *is* such a mass meeting; it goes on all the time, evolving the rules of the game. But in the larger and more complex societies we must delegate many social functions to representative persons and bodies. Their task is to maintain social order, manage, set standards, provide accreditation and so on. But, in principle, they should all of them be democratically accountable – provided that it be noted that what they are answerable to and should be checked against is not just a head-count, but rather the moving consensus of ordinary language and public opinion.

Radical democrats think that there is no more 'ultimate'

criterion, either of meaning, or truth, or value, than what is given within the moving consensus of ordinary language and daily life. In which case there are no 'absolutes',[6] and we should give up and try to live without ideas of unconditional or 'absolute' sovereignty, authority and allegiance. Above all, we should try to leave behind us all ideas of exclusive and unconditional allegiance to just one state, one ethnic group, or one religion.

I am concluding then that both in religion and in political life generally, we want to be rid of all ideas of monarchy, mystery, authority and exclusion. It is much better that *everything* should be on the level, freely negotiated and transparent. In such a world, it is much better for us to feel ourselves, and actually to be, of rather mixed and eclectic religious and political affiliation. In religion we should be wary of hierarchy and favour the 'broadest' churches and the most informal, creedless and democratic groups, such as the Congregational Union used to be and the Society of Friends still is.

I say this about hierarchy because hierarchy is government by a college of priests. A priest is not a charismatic figure who can innovate, but an institutionally-accredited person who is trained in a fixed body of knowledge and of ritual procedures. A priest is simply not expected to think, or to change anything; and if we are moving into a period of continual religious change in which religion, like art, will have to live by reinventing itself all the time, then it will be a period in which religious leadership will perforce be charismatic rather than priestly. The old coercive politics of belief will simply be abandoned as no longer workable.

So I picture a world in which reality itself is subject to continual renegotiation, and which is a radically democratic world. Perhaps religious movements in such a world may look like today's single-issue pressure-groups which appear and flourish in response to a suddenly-felt need. And perhaps Sea of Faith is itself the first church of the future.

We don't yet know how religious thought may be appraised

in times to come. As things are, religious thought is assessed purely juridically; that is, in terms of its political relation to one or more established orthodoxies. Anybody who attempts serious religious thought is automatically treated as being in the dock – by professional theologians! As yet, it seems that nobody has any idea of how to assess religious writing just on its own merits. Indeed, nobody wishes to attempt such assessment. But if it is the case that religion as quasi-political institution, in which truth is controlled by law, is now finally breaking down, then perhaps the time may come when at last people begin to care about religion, not as legal code and personal power-trip, but just *as religion*. I hope that day comes soon.

* * *

In retrospect, I see that I spent my life thinking about the relation between language and non-language, the topic which in the twentieth century replaced the old question of metaphysics.

I began by asking: How can statements about God have a truth value? How can language refer to God, be about God, describe God? Try again: How can our words *latch on* to God and *tell* us something about God? In response to this question, my turn towards the negative theology was bound to lead me out of metaphysics towards non-realism and towards a regulative view of statements seemingly about God. Generalizing the question of language, and asking how it manages to be 'about' *anything*, pitched me into the question of the relation of language to non-language. I found myself once again in Plato's Cave. Is language *itself* the Cave, and if so how can the prisoners in the Cave get to talk about an Outside? How can we access, or even *think*, non-language?

Early on, I phrased the question here as one about the relation between language and reality – a crude and unsatisfactory formulation, as I now see. It is much better, first to phrase the question in terms of the relation between language and non-language, and then to see it break up into four distinct sub-questions. What makes language *possible*? What is the *body* of language, what does it modulate or ride upon? What is it for a piece of language to be *about* this or that? and What is the *Other* of language, from which we differentiate it?

In the present essay I have proposed the answer: Non-language is Being. This cheers me up, by offering me a sort of synthesis and at least a temporary resting-place, because in the relation of language to Being I can find a unifying answer to the central question of philosophy – the question of metaphysics – and at the same time an answer also to the religious question, the question: What is the religious object?

To the philosophy of the future, and to the religion of the future we offer the formula: non-language is Being. And Being – what's that? Answer: Nobody can say, but this book was meant to be a sort of poem in praise of it.

Notes

Introduction: the story so far . . .

1. *After All* (1994); *The Last Philosophy* (1995); *Solar Ethics* (1995). All published in London by SCM Press. Earlier 'expressionist' books, from the same publisher, were *Creation out of Nothing* (1990), *What is a Story?* (1991) and *The Time Being* (1992). More recently, there have been *After God: the Future of Religion*, New York: Basic Books and London: Weidenfeld and Nicholson 1997 and *Mysticism After Modernity*, Oxford: Blackwell 1998.

2. The best one-volume introduction to Heidegger's work, with bibliographies, is Charles B. Guignon (ed.), *The Cambridge Companion to Heidegger*, Cambridge: Cambridge University Press 1993 by a strong team of scholars, mainly from North America.

3. 'Heidegger, contingency and pragmatism', in *Philosophical Papers Volume 2: Essays on Heidegger and Others*, Cambridge: Cambridge University Press 1991, pp.27–49.

4. See Reinhard May, *Heidegger's Hidden Sources: East Asian Influences on his Work* (1989); Eng. trans. Graham Parkes, London: Routledge 1996.

5. Cf. 'A Dialogue on Language', in his late *On the Way to Language* (1959); trans. Peter Hertz, New York: Harper and Row 1971.

1. What is Being?

1. I take this phrase from Michael Allen Gillespie's excellent *Hegel, Heidegger and the Ground of History*; but where does Heidegger himself use it? A version of it is printed, without a reference, on p.37 of David Farrell Krell (ed.), *Martin Heidegger: Basic Writings*, London: Routledge 1993:

We are too late for the gods
and too early for Being.

Being's poem, just begun, is man.

2. See John D. Caputo, 'Heidegger and Theology', in *The Cambridge Companion to Heidegger*, cited above, Introduction, n.2.

3. But we should express warm admiration for Stanley Rosen, *The Question of Being: A Reversal of Heidegger,* New Haven, Conn.: Yale University Press 1993.

4. This idea of a 'strong misreading' (Nietzsche, Bloom), a 'deviant recapitulation', and even an 'overcoming' (*Überwindung*: Heidegger himself, and Deleuze) has become widespread, and with good reason. The great philosophers of the past are sadly diminished if we are not allowed to approach them by any route other than orthodox critical-historical scholarship. Sometimes we need to battle against them, or to maltreat them. And it does them good.

5. In this fascinating text from Exodus, God seems to be portrayed as pure Being, pure transience. He won't allow Moses to see him head-on. Instead, he can only be seen disappearing. In the recent Everett Fox version (vv.22, 23):

> . . . when my Glory passes by,
> I will place you in the cleft of the rock
> and screen you with my hand
> until I have passed by.
> Then I will remove my hand;
> you shall see my back,
> but my face shall not be seen.

Such an equation of Isness, transience and divine Glory is very rare in the Western tradition, and very precious. ('Transient' is, in Latin, 'passing by'.)

6. In the old scholastic philosophy with which Heidegger was very familiar, there was a concept of being, and it was seen as undergirding the whole world of meaning. Thus Aquinas, *de Veritate*, q.1, art.1, teaches that being has one simple and formal concept: 'That which the intellect first conceives as the most-known and into which it resolves all its concepts is being . . . Hence it follows that all other concepts of the intellect are obtained by an addition to being.' Cajetan, like other scholastic philosophers, has some difficulty in reconciling this seemingly univocal concept of being with his doctrine of analogy. See

Thomas de Vio, Cardinal Cajetan, *The Analogy of Names and the Concept of Being*, trans. Edward A. Bushinski and Henry J. Koren, Pittsburgh, PA: Duquesne University 1959, pp.79ff.

The scholastic tradition, which went back ultimately to Aristotle, was a tradition of *dogmatic realism*; that is, it was assumed that all thinking is 'naturally' locked on to being. Being is itself the first and primal Meaning. For a brief exposition of some of the difficulties that result, see for example Anthony Kenny, *Aquinas*, Past Masters series, Oxford: Oxford University Press, 1980, c.2.

Like many or most other modern philosophers since Kant, Heidegger insists that the realms of Being and Meaning are distinct. 'Being is not a real predicate', says Kant; which means that Being ought not to be treated as a meaning. A language, a sign-system, is a system of interconnected meanings; but whether it applies to something cannot be ascertained internally. Being is therefore very appropriately put 'under erasure', Being, because it is a non-word, something outside and prior to language that we cannot think theoretically. We have no *concept* of being. Being, one might say, *feeds* language, *feeds* thinking. We should simply *wait upon* it.

7. Martin Heidegger, *An Introduction to Metaphysics*, a 1935 Freiburg lecture course, trans. Ralph Mannheim, New Haven, Conn.: Yale University Press 1959, 1987, p.61. This is a fairly clear work, albeit from Heidegger's period of most-open association with Nazism.

8. See Philippa Berry, 'Woman and Space according to Kristeva and Irigaray', in Berry and Andrew Wernick (eds), *Shadow of Spirit: Postmodernism and Religion*, London: Routledge 1992, pp.250–64.

9. See Martin Heidegger, *What is Called Thinking?*, a 1951–1952 Freiburg lecture course, trans. J. Glenn Gray, New York: Harper and Row 1968.

10. *The Question of Being*, cited above, n.3, p.291, etc.

2. *Being's time*

1. The Chinese character used in writing *ku/sunyata* suggests the sky. See Keiji Nishitani, *Religion and Nothingness*, trans. Jan Van Bragt, Berkeley: University of California Press 1982, p.296, s.v. 'EMPTINESS'. Nishitani studied with Heidegger in Freiburg from 1936–1939.

2. See Jacques Derrida, 'Violence and Metaphysics: An Essay on the Thought of Emmanuel Levinas', in *Writing and Difference* (1967);

translated by Alan Bass, London: Routledge 1978, c.4.

3. Michael Allen Gillespie, *Nihilism before Nietzsche*, Chicago: University of Chicago Press 1995, esp. c.1, well brings out the intellectual and moral destructiveness of theologies that stress the absolute sovereignty of the divine Will.

4. I first introduced the Fountain, as an image of Being and of the Eternal Return, in *After All*, pp.57–9. It was an image much used by Rilke.

5. Good studies of these figures, written in a way intelligible to people who read modern Western philosophy, are now becoming available. I particularly recommend Jay L. Garfield, *The Fundamental Wisdom of the Middle Way: Nagarjuna's Mulamadhyamakakarika*, New York: Oxford University Press 1995; and C.W. Huntington Jr, *The Emptiness of Emptiness: An Introduction to Early Indian Madhyamika*, Honolulu: University of Hawaii 1989.

6. Already, a great many people will say that they are content to 'go with the flow', and feel no need for absolutes or foundations. This may indicate that Heidegger's influence is already very widely diffused through our culture.

3. Be(coming)

1. Martin Heidegger, *The Question of Being* trans. by William Kluback and Jean T. Wilde, New York: Twayne 1958; London: Vision Press 1959. For Derrida's use of this theme, see Jacques Derrida, *Of Grammatology*, 1967; trans. Gayatri C. Spirak, Baltimore: Johns Hopkins University Press 1976, especially pp.xiv–xviii of the translator's preface.

2. Martin Heidegger, *On the Way to Language*, trans. Peter D. Hertz, New York: Harper and Row 1971, p.111.

3. There is a brief, clear introduction to this in Robin Le Poidevin, *Arguing for Atheism: An Introduction to the Philosophy of Religion*, London: Routledge 1996, pp.135–45. More detail in, for example, D.H. Mellor, *Real Time,* Cambridge: Cambridge University Press 1981.

4. Yuho Yokoi, *Zen Master Dogen: An Introduction with Selected Writings,* New York: Weatherhill 1976, Part Three, 4; pp.107–12.

5. Ibid., p.108.

6. Ibid., p.110.

4. Hap-hap-happy

1. The chief concern for the Reformers was with constructing a theology that could serve as the ideological background for the early modern state. They therefore pictured the Universe itself as a supremely efficiently-governed and moralistic totalitarian theocratic state. This doctrinal picture would then serve as a model for the exercise of social and religious authority in human society. It then seemed appropriate that both in nature and in society government was harshly punitive. Expectations were so low that 'the problem of evil' scarcely arose.

The modern problem of evil begins only in the later seventeenth century, when the rise of modern philosophy and natural science and the beginning of the Enlightenment had changed the agenda. Against the background of the new mechanistic world-picture, how could the enlightened individual recognize in the course of natural events the working out of a moral Providence? In a more humane epoch, people begin to ask why there has to be so much suffering.

John Hick, in *Evil and the God of Love,* London: Macmillan 1966, chapter VI, sect. 1, third footnote, and then continuing in c.VII, 1, rightly points to the influence of Ralph Cudworth's *True Intellectual System of the Universe* (1671). Cudworth – himself a Platonist – revived the old philosophical theodicy of Augustine and the neo-Platonists, and many of his arguments were subsequently adopted by William King in his *De Origine Mali* of 1702, and continued to be repeated until as recently as the 1960s. Since then, there has been a sudden collapse. We no longer want to ask the same questions about evil, and therefore have no interest in the old answers.

2. Friedrich Nietzsche, *The Twilight of the Idols and the Anti-Christ,* both 1888; trans. R.J. Hollingdale, London and New York: Penguin Books 1968, p.54.

5. Coming into the world

1. The preceding lines summarize a few themes of *Being and Time,* 1927; trans. John Macquarrie and Edward Robinson, Oxford: Basil Blackwell 1962.

2. Curiously, before the early twentieth century few philosophers raised the questions of what a world is, and why we believe that we have one. In *After God* (1997) I gave a 'political' answer: a world is a

realm, an ordered domain, all of whose denizens interact with each other and are subject to law. In short, the world is pictured on the model of the state, to which it gives cosmic backing. In which case 'the world' must have begun in neolithic times.

This political theory of 'the world' is no doubt compatible with the linguistic theory given in the present text. But notice a difference: the world of linguistic meaning is very large, hospitable, multi-dimensional and magical; whereas the world of our everyday social and public life is the 'true' world very much simplified and clarified, *in order to make it capable of being brought under the rule of Law.* In our public conversation, as in our science, our search for generality and consistency brings into being *the truth*, our world, the cosmos.

Artists and imaginative writers, then, are people who inhabit the big, original, magical and multi-dimensional world of linguistic meaning. People of affairs – scientists, lawyers, politicians and so on – inhabit a drastically reduced, coherent, law-governed version of the world.

The real world, the world of real beings, is then a rationalized, ordered subworld that has been extracted from the larger world of Meaning. Why was this extraction carried out? The motive was at first *political* (people needed to create ordered, law-governed societies) and later *scientific* (people needed to create ordered, law-governed bodies of knowledge).

6. Being and nihilism

1. The best-known European trickster is Till Eulenspiegel (Anglicized as 'Owl-glass'). The best known Amerindian trickster is the Winnebago one described in Paul Radin, *The Trickster,* London, Routledge 1956; New York: Schocken Books 1972, a volume which also contains C.G. Jung's essay on the Trickster's psychology. For this latter aspect, see also Mary Douglas, in *Purity and Danger,* Harmondsworth: Penguin 1966; London: Routledge, Ark 1984, c.5. See also Enid Welsford, *The Fool,* London: Faber 1935, along with Paul V.A. Williams (ed.), *The Fool and the Trickster: Studies in Honour of Enid Welsford,* Cambridge: D.S. Brewer 1979.

2. The American historian of philosophy Richard H. Popkin is probably still the best guide to the Sceptical tradition. But the Sceptic, like the Trickster, always tends to fall into neglect. He threatens to undermine academic values, and therefore lacks the academic advo-

cates who are needed nowadays if one is to survive. But see Peter Burke, *Montaigne*, Oxford: Oxford University Press 1981, esp. cc.3, 4 and bibliographies thereto.

3. Hilary Lawson, *Reflexivity: the Postmodern Predicament*, London: Hutchinson 1985.

7. Being and language

1. Gaston Diehl, *Vasarely*, trans. Eileen B. Hennessy, New York: Crown Publishers 1979, e.g. pp.14, 17, 20, 22, 23.

2. See *The Will to Power*, New York: Random House 1968, Kaufmann numbering, nos. 70, 481, 556, 604.

3. Richard Rorty's many excellent papers, collected in *Consequences of Pragmatism*, Brighton: Harvester Press 1982 and in *Objectivity, Relativism and Truth: Philosophical Papers Volume 1*, Cambridge: Cambridge University Press 1991, bear eloquent witness to the political pressure that bears upon non-realists. Some philosophers, like Hilary Putnam and Mary Hesse, continue to use the term 'realism' in connection with their own position, even though they are very far from the traditional *metaphysical* sort of realism. Others, like Rorty himself, try to shift the terminological ground. Rorty says he's not a realist, but a pragmatist and an anti-representationalist. As for 'relativism', Rorty's tactic is simply to accept the loony-Right definition of the word – 'every belief on a certain topic, or perhaps about any topic, is as good as every other' – and to say that of course 'no one holds this view' (*Consequences*, p.166).

Thus Putnam and Hesse set out to undermine realism from a position nominally *inside* it; and Rorty teaches relativism from a position nominally *outside* it. The need to resort to such defensive strategies shows how violent people's convictions are in these matters.

4. Interestingly, the empty non-realist vision of the world that I have been describing is very close indeed to that described by some Christian theologians. Thus, for Rudolf Bultmann, to believe in God as Creator is to see the world as created, which in turn is to see that it is nothing in itself but mere transient contingency:

> We must become clear that to say of anything in the world that it is God's creature is at the same time to say that in and of itself it is nothing. What is created does not have its own existence . . .
>
> We understand the world as God's creation only when we know

about this nothingness that encompasses every created thing; only when, beyond all the importance that the creatures can acquire for us, we do not forget the final unimportance that stamps them as creatures; only when, beyond all of the world's beauty that may charm us, we do not forget the shadow of nothing that lies over every splendid thing and constantly seeks to remind us of its transitoriness . . .

These words are from the sermon 'Faith in God the Creator', delivered at Marburg in 1934, and reprinted in *Existence and Faith*, trans. Schubert M. Ogden, London: Hodder and Stoughton 1961.

Bultmann and Heidegger had been close colleagues at Marburg during the years 1923–1928. Bultmann saw in *Being and Time* a rationalized and demythologized account of the Protestant view of the world and of our life, and took it up with enthusiasm.

8. *The reciprocal production of being and meaning*

1. Compare the account in this chapter with that given in *After All* and *The Last Philosophy*, where I several times set up a circular relationship between our continual making of the world, and the world's continual making of us. But here I am pointing to a supplement or remainder.

9. *Being's law*

1. This chapter has argued emphatically that *we* invented all the cosmologies; *we* opened all the slots for Being to fill. A large, historically-evolved and rather miscellaneous accumulation of human habits, customs and traditions, acts as Being's law.

To put it another way, the world is so plastic that it is evidently capable of being constructed or shaped in a great variety of different ways, and the situation is that we cannot clearly distinguish between our own habitual ways of organizing the world, and the world's own habitual ways of organizing itself. And if we cannot make the distinction, then in effect we have to say simply that our language games are Being's law.

Scientific realists are very displeased about this. They don't object very much to the suggestion that the ordinary person's cosmology comes down at last to a collection of old wives' tales, but they are most insistent that their own highly-evolved mathematical physics is a body of objective – even 'absolute' – knowledge, different in kind from the world-view of everyday life.

This is exactly like the religious fundamentalist's claim that *his* religious language moves in a pure and exalted region in which words have uniquely clear, fixed and God-guaranteed meanings, and which is free from all the frailties and relativities of ordinary human speech. And in both cases the claim to have altogether transcended ordinariness and to have achieved absolute or objective knowledge is mythical. For in both cases the high-level specialized vocabulary presupposes and rests upon the ordinariness in which we all begin, and the ordinary language that we all learnt first. Physics does not go all the way down to the ground: it goes down only into ordinariness. The grand high-level general claims (religious doctrines, or physical theories) are in both cases demonstrably human historical products, and when they are tested in the laboratory, or applied in life – as they must be – again, they are referred back to and checked against the ordinariness in which all begins and ends. The scientist who in a laboratory performs an experiment to test a theory still in doing so presupposes the ordinary construction of the spatio-temporal world and the ordinary evidence of the senses. We have no access to the testimony of any disembodied ideal observer: we are stuck in, and stuck with, ordinariness. Thus all claims to have wholly transcended ordinary language and the ordinary construction of the world, whether scientific or religious, are mythical, and are put forward in order to gain power and authority. The philosophical situation remains that our untidy, historically-evolved ordinariness is Being's law. Which is why we speak of Being as our partner, and of 'cosmic humanism'.

10. *Being and Technology*

1. The odd Platonic dream of a superior kind of knowledge that makes you into a superior kind of person, a philosopher-king, today attracts some scientists. But it gives rise to paradoxes, which are particularly acute for our evangelical Darwinians. For, if the Darwinian theory of human origins which they profess is correct, and if it has the wide-ranging implications for human life and thought which they claim, it must tend to undermine itself, and their claims. From a Darwinian point of view, one can understand that animals like us should have evolved sense-organs, emotions, cognitive abilities and so forth that are relevant to our survival; but how can natural selection

give rise to radically supra-biological beings, god-like spectators of all time and existence, and equipped with 'absolute' or objective knowledge of reality? Thoroughgoing Darwinism consorts readily enough with pragmatism; but how can it be reconciled with strong metaphysical realism?

I conclude that a lowly theory of human origins, held in a pragmatic spirit and with due regard for the primacy of ordinariness, is fine and entirely self-consistent. But if it is made into a new theology, or a new philosophical superscience, then it must refute itself.

2. Frank J. Tipler, *The Physics of Immortality: Modern Cosmology, God and the Resurrection of the Dead*, New York: Doubleday 1994; London: Macmillan 1995, argues that in the computers of the far future the divine Mind will become conscious of itself, and the dead will be raised. Some well-known figures endorsed the book!

3. Heidegger's best known essay on technology is the title-piece in *The Question Concerning Technology and Other Essays*, trans. William Lovitt, New York: Harper Torchbooks 1977. There he describes 'the essence of technology' as 'Enframing' (*Gestell*). By this he means 'the ordering of everything as standing-reserve': modern global technology treats all reality, everything, as potential raw material, held in reserve until it is required for exploitation.

The connection between the ambitions of technology and the attributes of God is ancient and mythological, but the young Hegel makes an interesting argument out of it. He pictures the Hebrew Patriarchs as threatened by violent natural forces, and battling to survive in a world of which they understood little. They tried to imagine what that Power must be like that could fully understand and control Nature. This led them to postulate a God who was all-knowing and all-powerful, the Lord of Nature. By worshipping and serving him they might gain a share in his absolute knowledge and control of the world. See G.W.F. Hegel, *On Christianity: Early Theological Writings*, trans. T.M. Knox and R. Kroner, New York: Harper Torchbooks 1961, p.183.

What is striking about this argument is not just its suggestion that technology is motivated by a desire to gain the divine attributes for men, but the bolder and deeper idea that theology itself is technologically motivated.

11. *Being and the end of thinking*

1. See, for example, Daniel W. Hardy in David F. Ford (ed.), *The Modern Theologians*, Volume II, Oxford: Blackwell 1989, p.60.

12. *Human Being*

1. Michael E. Zimmerman, 'Heidegger, Buddhism and Deep Ecology', in Charles Guignon (ed.), *The Cambridge Companion to Heidegger* (cited above, Introduction, n.2), pp.26off.

2. *Tractatus*, 6.45 and 6.5, 6.522.

3. Compare Wittgenstein's return into ordinariness with Kierkegaard's return into 'immediacy after reflection', and Hume's return from his sceptical reflections into common life. These philosophers – and many others, including Nagarjuna – do not see philosophy, or even religious belief, as radically changing the way we see things. Rather, the detour through speculative philosophy or through religious thought and practice is therapeutic. It cures a feeling of distress or discomfort that was troubling us. It helps us to return more cheerfully into ordinariness, and to affirm it.

My advisor instructs me to add a postscript: Kierkegaard's return into ordinariness is rather different from that of either Hume or Wittgenstein. Kierkegaard's return to ordinariness is achieved *by faith*; and faith has its own proper tension. It keeps one a little keyed up, stretched. I am reminded that elsewhere I have myself called this tension 'anguish'.

4. On Heidegger's debt to St Paul, see Brian D. Ingraffia, *Postmodern Theory and Biblical Theology: Vanquishing God's Shadow*, Cambridge: Cambridge University Press 1995, Part II, pp.101–64.

13. *No Object*

1. See my *Mysticism After Modernity*, Blackwell 1997, c.7, pp.93–103.

2. There are earlier versions of the ideas here presented in *The Long-Legged Fly* (1987) and *The Time Being* (1992). My ideas are indebted to, amongst others, Mary Douglas and Gilles Deleuze.

3. P.4 above.

4. C.6, note 1 above.

5. From the Metta Sutta: *Sutta-Nipata* 1,8. I am indebted to Caroline Cupitt for this reference.

Notes

14. The way to Being

1. II Corinthians 4.16, AV: more recent translations, here as so often elsewhere, substitute euphemisms for Paul's plain words.

2. My main previous attempts at a postmodern spirituality are *Life Lines* (1986) and *Solar Ethics* (1995).

3. I first learned the idea that one should treat complexity as prior, and the simple as a reduction of it, from the ethnomusicologist Laurence Picken.

4. Once again, I express gratitude to Jean-Jacques Lecercle for his very valuable book on Deleuze: *Philosophy through the Looking-Glass: Language, Nonsense, Desire,* London: Hutchinson 1985.

5. David Hume, *A Treatise of Human Nature*, ed. L.A. Selby-Bigge, Oxford: Clarendon Press 1888. See the analytical index, s.v. 'Custom', pp.655ff.

6. Richard Peters, *Hobbes,* Harmondsworth: Penguin 1956, makes some of the right points here. Like Heidegger, Hobbes makes a distinction between those beings that have a world, and those beings that merely figure in a world. He wonders how it is 'that some natural bodies have in themselves the patterns almost of all things, and others of none at all' (Peters, p.85, quoting the *De Corpore*).

7. See above, p.29.

8. Lucretius, *The Nature of the Universe*, trans. R.E. Latham, Harmondsworth: Penguin 1951.

9. Martin Heidegger, *What is Called Thinking?*, trans. by J. Glenn Gray, New York: Harper and Row, Colophon Books 1968.

10. Op.cit., pp.240–4 (from Part II, Lecture XI).

11. G.S. Kirk and J.E. Raven, *The Presocratic Philosophers,* Cambridge: Cambridge University Press 1957, p.269 (i.e., 344, last line). In the past I have usually supposed that Parmenides' doctrine here is to be read as a piece of metaphysical dogma. But I now see that it may be open to a mystical reading.

15. Being's poem

1. Hans Küng, *Does God Exist? An Answer for Today,* London: Collins 1978.

2. David Hume, *Dialogues Concerning Natural Religion*, Part XII, Oxford; Oxford University Press, World's Classics edition, ed. J.C.A. Gaskin, 1993. PHILO's speech, pp.118–21.

3. German: Bern: A. Francke Verlag 1947. See *Martin Heidegger:*

Basic Writings (cited above, c.1, n.1), pp.214–65.

4. An element of planning, however, did enter into *After All* (1993), written at a time when I was in extremely poor health, both mentally and physically. The real topic of the book was a few moments of happiness so great that for their sakes it was permissible to set out to make the entire book happy.

5. Graham McCann, *Cary Grant: A Class Apart*, London: Fourth Estate 1996, p.18.

16. Faith in Being

1. See *Mysticism After Modernity*, cited in c.13, n.1 above.

2. See Coleridge's *Collected Works*, London: Routledge and Princeton: Princeton University Press no.11, vol.II, 1995, p.834.

3. I introduced the idea of *solar* living in the 1994/5 works cited in the introduction, n.1. Best summary is *After God*, London: Weidenfeld and Nicholson 1997, pp.89f.

4. If there can be faith in Being, what is *un*faith; what is the religion of Being's equivalent of unbelief? The question is prompted by Damien Hirst's book, *I Want to Spend the Rest of my Life Everywhere, with Everyone, One to One, Always, Forever, Now*, London: Booth-Clibborn editions 1997. Hirst is obsessed with transience, death and medical horrors. His work is brilliant as a protest against the fatuous optimism of our late-capitalist consumer culture. But he stops well short of affirming Being, and surely *might* therefore be interpreted as a fiercely pessimistic and 'black' artist.

Inconclusion

1. The title of *The Time Being* contained allusions to Auden's 'Christmas Oratorio' *For the Time Being*, Dōgen's *uji* or 'being-time', and also to Heidegger's *Being and Time*. So the affinity with Heidegger was beginning to dawn on me as long ago as early 1991, when the book was written.

2. *Journal of Theological Studies*, NS XVIII, Part I (April 1967), pp.104–26.

3. The view that mediaeval philosophical theology was eventually brought to something like systematic completion only in and by Spinoza was well stated by A.O. Lovejoy in *The Great Chain of Being*, Cambridge, Mass.: Harvard University Press 1936.

4. The classic example, in Lloyd Morgan and other early-twentieth-century biological theorists, was the evolution of the horse, from its dog-sized and many-toed ancestor Eohippus to the modern horse. But the question arises: does the apparent straight-line development exist out-there, or has it been created by the way paleontologists have arranged their specimens? Has the straight line been produced by natural selection, or by selection in museums?

5. Numbers 11.29. 'Don't be jealous for my sake!', says Moses generously. He is glad to see religious power dispersed.

6. Anti-relativists who believe in 'absolutes' should check out the views held in different societies, and in different historical periods, about just what these 'absolutes' are supposed to be. They'll soon realize that just as nothing dates quicker than science-fiction dreams of the future, so nothing is more relative than a people's 'absolutes', and nothing is more fragile and disputable than a 'certainty'.

Index of names

Index